HO CI

MINH CITY

TRAVEL

GUIDE 2024

Discover the Vibrant Culture, Delicious Cuisine, and Rich History of Vietnam's Bustling Metropolis

Anthony Bolds

HO CHI MINH CITY MAP

SACN THIS CODE TO ACCESS THE MAP

TABLE OF CONTENTS

HO CHI MINH CITY MAP 3

INTRODUCTION TO HO CHI MINH CITY 11

HISTORY AND OVERVIEW 12

CULTURAL SIGNIFICANCE 15

CLIMATE AND BEST TIME TO VISIT 17

CHAPTER 1 21

GETTING TO HO CHI MINH CITY 21

INTERNATIONAL AND DOMESTIC FLIGHTS.................. 21

VISA AND ENTRY REQUIREMENTS 24

TRANSPORTATION FROM THE AIRPORT....................... 26

CHAPTER 2 29

ACCOMMODATION OPTIONS 29

LUXURY HOTELS.. 29

MID-RANGE HOTELS 32

BUDGET HOSTELS AND GUESTHOUSES........................ 35

UNIQUE STAYS (BOUTIQUE HOTELS, HOMESTAYS)... 37

CHAPTER 3 41

NAVIGATING THE CITY 41

PUBLIC TRANSPORTATION (BUSES, METRO) 41

TAXIS AND RIDE-SHARING SERVICES 43

RENTING MOTORBIKES AND BICYCLES 45

WALKING TOURS 47

CHAPTER 4 49

TOP ATTRACTIONS 49

HISTORICAL SITES (REUNIFICATION PALACE, WAR
REMNANTS MUSEUM)... 49

RELIGIOUS SITES (NOTRE-DAME CATHEDRAL
BASILICA, JADE EMPEROR PAGODA) 52

MODERN LANDMARKS (BITEXCO FINANCIAL TOWER,
LANDMARK 81) 53

CULTURAL SITES (HO CHI MINH CITY MUSEUM, FINE
ARTS MUSEUM) 55

CHAPTER 5 57

NEIGHBORHOODS TO EXPLORE................................ 57

DISTRICT 1: THE HEART OF THE CITY 57

DISTRICT 3: COLONIAL ARCHITECTURE AND LOCAL
VIBES 59

DISTRICT 5: CHOLON (CHINATOWN) 61

DISTRICT 7: MODERN URBAN LIVING 63

CHAPTER 6 65

CULINARY EXPERIENCES 65

STREET FOOD HIGHLIGHTS.............................. 65

MUST-TRY DISHES (PHO, BANH MI, GOI CUON)........... 67

BEST RESTAURANTS AND EATERIES............................ 69

COOKING CLASSES AND FOOD TOURS 73

CHAPTER 7 75

SHOPPING GUIDE.. 75

TRADITIONAL MARKETS (BEN THANH MARKET, BINH TAY MARKET) 75

MODERN MALLS (SAIGON CENTRE, VINCOM CENTER) 76

LOCAL BOUTIQUES AND ARTISAN SHOPS 79

SOUVENIRS TO BUY 81

CHAPTER 8 85

NIGHTLIFE AND ENTERTAINMENT 85

BARS AND PUBS 85

NIGHTCLUBS AND LIVE MUSIC VENUES 88

THEATERS AND CINEMAS 92

NIGHT MARKETS AND EVENING ACTIVITIES.............. 96

CHAPTER 9 99

DAY TRIPS AND EXCURSIONS 99

MEKONG DELTA 99

CU CHI TUNNELS 102

VUNG TAU BEACH 104

CAN GIO BIOSPHERE RESERVE 107

CHAPTER 10 109

CULTURAL ETIQUETTE AND TIPS.................... 109

DO'S AND DON'TS 109

DON'TS 111

LOCAL CUSTOMS AND TRADITIONS............... 112

ESSENTIAL VIETNAMESE PHRASES 115

CHAPTER 11 119

PRACTICAL INFORMATION 119

CURRENCY AND BANKING............................... 119

HEALTH AND SAFETY TIPS.............................. 122

INTERNET AND SIM CARDS.............................. 125

CONCLUSION.. 128

INTRODUCTION TO HO CHI MINH CITY

As an enthusiastic traveler and seasoned novelist, I've seen innumerable cities, each with its beauty and tale. However, few places have captured my heart and imagination like Ho Chi Minh City. This thriving metropolis, formerly known as Saigon, is a colorful tapestry of history, culture, and modernity. It's a city where ancient temples coexist with sleek skyscrapers, where echoes from the past mingle effortlessly with the pulse of the present.

During my several travels to Ho Chi Minh City, I discovered hidden gems, ate delicious street cuisine, and immersed myself in the city's complex network of districts. Every area of this city has a tale to tell, from the frantic energy of Ben Thanh Market to the tranquil beauty of the Saigon River.

This travel guide is more than simply a list of advice and recommendations; it's also a personal account of my trips and discoveries. It's designed to help you navigate Ho Chi Minh City like a local, providing insights that only come from genuinely understanding a place. Whether you're a first-time visitor or a seasoned tourist, this guide will help you discover the heart of the city and make the most of your trip.

Join me as we explore the bustling streets, sample the varied flavors, and learn about the rich history and culture that make Ho Chi Minh City unlike any other location. Together, we'll discover the mysteries of this incredible city, making every moment of your journey unforgettable. Welcome to Ho Chi Minh City! Let the journey begin!

HISTORY AND OVERVIEW

Originally a tranquil town along the Saigon River, the area expanded in the 17th century when Vietnamese inhabitants moved southward. Named after Vietnam's mythological progenitor, King Hung, the city was formerly part of the Khmer Empire and known as Prey Nokor. The Vietnamese influence spread, and by the 18th century, the city had developed into an important commerce hub known as Gia Dinh.

The French occupied Vietnam in the mid-nineteenth century, and in 1859, Saigon was taken and made the capital of French Indochina. This time saw significant urban growth, with French architecture, vast boulevards, and contemporary infrastructure that continue to shape the city's landscape today. The Notre Dame Cathedral, the Saigon Central Post Office, and the Ben Thanh Market are all prominent landmarks from this era, combining Western architecture with indigenous materials and styles.

Following World War II, Vietnam's battle for independence resulted in the end of French colonial rule. The Geneva Accords of 1954 divided Vietnam into North and South, with Saigon serving as the capital of South Vietnam. The city had fast economic growth and became a focal point during the Vietnam War, representing resistance and the desire for freedom.

The end of the war in 1975 signaled the start of a new chapter. Saigon was renamed Ho Chi Minh City to honor the revolutionary leader Ho Chi Minh, who was instrumental in Vietnam's reunification efforts. The city's reunification encouraged attempts to repair and modernize, overcoming the devastation caused by decades of conflict.

Today, Ho Chi Minh City is a thriving economic and cultural hub. Skyscrapers rise among old buildings, resulting in a distinct skyline that represents both the city's rich heritage and future aspirations. The city's population is diversified, consisting of ethnic Vietnamese, Chinese, and expats from all over the world, who contribute to a complex tapestry of cultures and customs.

The city's culinary scene reflects this diversity. Ho Chi Minh City's flavors range from street food booths to upmarket restaurants, with both traditional and contemporary options. Local favorites include pho, banh mi, and fresh spring rolls, but international cuisines are also widely accessible, appealing to global preferences.

Ho Chi Minh City's expansion extends beyond its physical and economic dimensions. It is a hub for education and innovation, with multiple colleges and research facilities that encourage a culture of learning and advancement. The city's innovation and startup industry is fast booming, attracting investors and entrepreneurs looking to capitalize on its dynamic market.

Despite its fast industrialization, Ho Chi Minh City is nevertheless firmly rooted in its cultural heritage. Festivals, traditional music, and art flourish, honoring the city's legacy. Landmarks like as the War Remnants Museum and the Reunification Palace provide insights into the city's history, helping both locals and visitors better comprehend it.

Ho Chi Minh City residents are noted for their resilience, kindness, and entrepreneurial spirit. Their ability to adapt and thrive throughout times of change and misfortune is a defining feature of the city. Ho Chi Minh City continues to expand and evolve, but it remains a location where history and modernity mix, providing a unique and exciting experience for all visitors.

CULTURAL SIGNIFICANCE

Ho Chi Minh City's cultural significance revolves around its historical legacy. The city played an important role during the Vietnam War, which is commemorated by different sites and museums. The War Remnants Museum provides a moving glimpse at the war's impact, while the Reunification Palace, where the Vietnam War ended, serves as a symbol of the country's perseverance and unity.

The city's architecture reflects its imperial origins and quick urbanization. French colonial architecture, such as the Notre Dame Cathedral Basilica and the Central Post Office, contrast well with the modern skyscrapers that now dominate the skyline. These architectural marvels offer an insight into the city's development and fusion of Eastern and Western influences.

Ho Chi Minh City's cultural landscape is influenced by its diverse population. The city is home to a variety of ethnic communities, each adding to its vibrant cultural tapestry. This diversity is particularly seen in the city's food scene. From traditional Vietnamese meals like pho and banh mi to a wide range of other cuisines, the city's food culture reflects its vibrant and welcoming attitude.

Traditional marketplaces, like as Ben Thanh Market, provide a real shopping experience for travelers, offering everything from local handicrafts to fresh fruit. These markets are more than just places to purchase; they are also public areas that showcase local culture and daily life.

The arts contribute significantly to the city's cultural identity. The Saigon Opera House, a spectacular specimen of French colonial architecture, accommodates a wide range of acts, including classical music and contemporary dance. The city's vibrant art scene is also evident in its various galleries and street art, which highlight the originality and innovation of local artists.

Festivals and festivals are central to the city's cultural life. Tet, the Vietnamese Lunar New Year, is the most important celebration, with colorful parades, traditional music, and family gatherings. The Mid-Autumn Festival and other religious events throughout the year highlight the city's rich cultural heritage.

The educational and cultural institutions of Ho Chi Minh City demonstrate the city's commitment to conserving its historic legacy while embracing modernization. The Museum of Vietnamese History and the Fine Arts Museum are just two examples of sites where the city's past and present intersect to educate and excite both residents and visitors.

Climate of Ho Chi Minh City

There are two different seasons in Ho Chi Minh City's tropical climate: dry and wet.

During the dry season (December-April), the city gets high temperatures and little to no rainfall. The coolest months are December through February, when temperatures range from 70°F to 90°F. These months are especially nice, with low humidity and chilly evenings. Temperatures soar in March and April, reaching the mid-90s°F, but the lack of rain makes exploring the city and its surroundings easier.

The rainy season, lasting from May to November, is characterized by frequent and severe downpours, particularly from June to August. However, these showers are usually brief, happening in the late afternoon or evening, and rarely last all day. Despite the rain, temperatures remain high, ranging from 75°F to 95°F. Humidity levels are also higher during this time, making the weather appear warmer than it is.

The best time to visit

The best time to visit Ho Chi Minh City is during the dry season, which runs from December to February. Here's why certain months are ideal for your trip.

Cooler temperatures and decreased humidity enhance the tourist experience. You may comfortably tour the city's sights, such as the Notre-Dame Cathedral Basilica of Saigon, the War Remnants Museum, and the bustling Bến Thành Market, without the discomfort of extreme heat or sudden rain showers.

Tet Festival, the Vietnamese Lunar New Year, takes place throughout January or February, creating a festive atmosphere. This is Vietnam's most important holiday, and the city comes alive with colorful decorations, traditional performances, and a celebratory atmosphere. Experiencing Tet in Ho Chi Minh City offers a unique perspective on Vietnamese culture and traditions.

Clear skies during the dry season provide ideal conditions for photography and panoramic views of the city from famous locations such as the Bitexco Financial Tower Sky Deck. The lack of rain also facilitates day visits to local sights such as the Cu Chi Tunnels and the Mekong Delta.

Tips for Travelers

Stay Hydrated: Even in the dry season, the heat can be extreme. Carry a water bottle to remain hydrated while exploring.

Wear Light Clothing: Lightweight, breathable textiles are perfect for warm temperatures. To protect yourself from the sun, remember to wear a hat and sunscreen.

Plan for Rain in the Wet Season: If you visit during the rainy season, carry a lightweight raincoat or umbrella. Plan indoor activities or trips to museums and markets that will be unaffected by the weather.

CHAPTER 1

GETTING TO HO CHI MINH CITY

INTERNATIONAL AND DOMESTIC FLIGHTS

International flights

Ho Chi Minh City is well connected to major cities across the world via Tan Son Nhat International Airport (SGN), Vietnam's busiest airport. Whether you are flying from North America, Europe, Asia, or Australia, various airlines offer direct and connecting flights to Ho Chi Minh City.

From North America: Major airlines such as American Airlines, United Airlines, and Delta fly from Los Angeles, San Francisco, and New York. While direct flights are restricted, layovers in locations like Tokyo, Seoul, and Hong Kong make the journey easier.

European passengers can select from several airlines, including Air France, British Airways, and Lufthansa. Direct flights are accessible from major hubs including Paris, London, and Frankfurt. These airlines frequently give good service and amenities, resulting in a nice experience.

From Asia: Due to the proximity, flights from other Asian countries are frequent and often direct. Singapore Airlines, Cathay Pacific, and Thai Airways operate regular flights from Singapore, Hong

Kong, and Bangkok. These short flights make regional travel to Ho Chi Minh City simple and efficient.

Travelers from Australia can book direct flights with carriers such as Qantas and Vietnam carriers from Sydney and Melbourne. The flight time is normally around eight hours, making it suitable for a long weekend or prolonged vacation.

Domestic flights

Vietnam's internal aircraft network is robust, making Ho Chi Minh City easily accessible from throughout the country. Domestic airlines such as Vietnam Airlines, VietJet Air, and Bamboo Airways operate frequent flights to SGN.

From Hanoi: The capital city of Hanoi is around two hours distant by air. With multiple flights operating daily, it is simple to pick a comfortable time to travel. The route is served by all major domestic airlines, ensuring low fares and frequent options.

From Da Nang: Da Nang, in central Vietnam, is another popular departure point. The flight time to Ho Chi Minh City is around one hour and twenty minutes. Airlines offer many flights throughout the day, making it simple to organize travel plans.

From Phu Quoc: Flights to Ho Chi Minh City take around one hour. This route is served by several airlines, giving you a choice in scheduling your departure.

Other Cities: Ho Chi Minh City is easily accessible from several other Vietnamese cities, including Nha Trang, Hue, and Can Tho. Domestic flights are often inexpensive and frequent, making air travel a practical way to explore various parts of Vietnam.

Tips for Booking Flights

Book early: Flight rates might fluctuate dramatically depending on demand. Booking your tickets far in advance can help you get the greatest deals.

Flexible Dates: If you have flexible trip dates, use ticket comparison tools to identify the cheapest days to fly. Mid-week flights are frequently less expensive than those on weekends.

Check airlines: Different airlines provide varying levels of service and amenities. Researching customer evaluations and in-flight offerings might assist ensure a positive trip.

Travel Light: Many airlines have stringent luggage regulations. Traveling with only a carry-on can save time and money, especially on low-cost carriers.

Stay updated: Flight schedules are subject to change, so keep an eye out for any airline updates on your journey.

VISA AND ENTRY REQUIREMENTS

Visa requirements

The visa requirements for Vietnam, including Ho Chi Minh City, differ depending on your nationality and the purpose of your visit. Here's a simple guide to help you through the process:

Visa-Free Entry: Citizens from selected countries can enter Vietnam without a visa for short visits. This period can last from 14 to 90 days, depending on your nationality. For example, nationals of ASEAN nations such as Thailand, Malaysia, Singapore, Indonesia, and the Philippines can enter Vietnam without a visa for up to 30 days. Citizens of Japan, South Korea, and several European countries can remain without a visa for 15 to 90 days.

Vietnam offers an e-visa system to people from 80 countries, including the US, Canada, Australia, and the UK. The e-visa is valid for a single entry and a stay of up to thirty days. The application process is straightforward and may be done online. You will need to complete an application form, upload a passport-sized photo, and give a scanned copy of your passport. Once authorized, you will receive the e-visa by email.

Travelers arriving in Vietnam by plane can obtain a Visa on Arrival (VOA). To receive a VOA, first apply for a permission letter from a travel agency or online service. With this letter, you can obtain your visa at one of Vietnam's international airports upon arrival. This visa is valid for both single and multiple entries, with durations ranging from 30 to 90 days.

To obtain a visa in advance of your trip, apply at a Vietnamese embassy or consulate in your home country. This process includes submitting your passport, a completed application form, passport-sized pictures, and the visa fees. Processing times may vary, so apply well in advance of your travel date.

Entry Requirements:

Ensure your passport is valid for at least six months beyond your scheduled arrival date in Vietnam. This is a standard requirement for foreign travel and helps to prevent issues at the border.

Documentation of Exit: Although not usually required, it is recommended to have documentation of further travel, such as a return ticket or ticket to another location. Immigration agents may request to see this as confirmation that you do not intend to overstay your visa.

Recent health restrictions may require tourists to complete a health declaration form. Before your journey, make sure to verify if any vaccines are advised or required. The CDC and WHO give up-to-date travel health information.

TRANSPORTATION FROM THE AIRPORT

When you arrive at Tan Son Nhat International Airport in Ho Chi Minh metropolis, you find a dynamic and bustling metropolis brimming with vitality. With a few choices available, getting from the airport to your destination in the city can be simple and seamless.

Taxi Services: Taxis are one of the most convenient and popular modes of transportation from the airport to the city center. There are several reliable taxi companies at the airport, including Vinasun and Mai Linh. These cabs are frequently parked directly outside the arrival terminal. Always keep the taxi meter running to avoid any confusion regarding the fare. A drive to District 1, the heart of Ho Chi Minh City, usually takes 20 to 30 minutes, depending on traffic, and costs between 150,000 and 200,000 VND (about $7 to $10 USD).

Ride-Hailing applications: Another current and convenient option is to use ride-hailing applications such as Grab or Gojek. These apps let you book a car or motorcycle ride right from your smartphone. Simply download the app, enter your pickup location, and select your destination. The fare is computed in advance, ensuring openness and avoiding the need to negotiate with the driver. This option is very useful if you prefer cashless transactions.

Airport Shuttle Buses: For those searching for a less expensive means to get to the city, airport shuttle buses are an excellent option. The Airport Bus 109 connects Tan Son Nhat Airport to 23/9 Park in District 1. The buses are air-conditioned and pleasant, with a direct route to the city center. The fare is approximately 20,000 VND (less than $1 USD), making it a cost-effective option. Buses run every 15-20 minutes, so you won't have to wait long.

Public buses: If you're going light and not in a hurry, public buses are an even more affordable option to get to the city. Bus number 152, for example, connects the airport to Ben Thanh Market in District 1. While this alternative is fairly inexpensive, it might be busy and slow due to the several stops along the way. However, it is a fantastic method to get a sense of the local commute.

Private Transfers: If you want a more personalized and pleasant ride, private transfer services are available. These can be reserved in advance online or through a travel agency. A driver will greet you at the arrivals gate, assist you with your bags, and transport you directly to your hotel or any other location in the city. While more expensive, this alternative offers peace of mind and a stress-free experience, particularly after a long travel.

Motorbike Taxis: If you're traveling alone and don't have much luggage, motorbike taxis (known as "xe om") are a speedy and exciting way to reach to your destination. They are commonly available throughout the airport. Ensure that the fare is agreed upon ahead of time, or use ride-hailing apps to arrange one. This choice provides a quick and exhilarating ride through the downtown traffic.

Automobile Rentals: For those who like to explore the city and its surroundings at their leisure, automobile rental options are available at the airport. Driving in Ho Chi Minh City might be difficult due to severe traffic and varying driving behaviors, but it is an alternative for people who are comfortable navigating congested streets.

CHAPTER 2

ACCOMMODATION OPTIONS

LUXURY HOTELS

1. The Reverie Saigon

Located in the heart of District 1, The Reverie Saigon is renowned for its opulent design and unparalleled service. This hotel combines Italian sophistication with Vietnamese charm, providing guests with an extraordinary stay. The rooms and suites are exquisitely decorated with lavish furnishings, offering stunning views of the city or the Saigon River.

Price Range: $300 - $600 per night

Location: Ho Chi Minh City's District 1, 22–36 Nguyen Hue Boulevard

Contact: +84 28 3823 6688

2. Park Hyatt Saigon

Park Hyatt Saigon offers an elegant retreat in the bustling city center. This hotel is known for its colonial architecture and contemporary interiors. Guests can enjoy spacious rooms, a beautiful outdoor pool, and exceptional dining options. The hotel also offers personalized services to ensure a memorable stay.

Price Range: $250 - $500 per night

Location: Ho Chi Minh City's District 1, 2 Lam Son Square

Contact: +84 28 3824 1234

3. InterContinental Saigon

The InterContinental Saigon stands out for its modern luxury and strategic location. Situated near key landmarks, it offers easy access to shopping, dining, and cultural attractions. The hotel features elegant rooms, a state-of-the-art fitness center, and multiple dining venues that cater to various tastes.

Price Range: $200 - $450 per night

Location: Corner of Hai Ba Trung Street & Le Duan Boulevard, District 1, Ho Chi Minh City

Contact: +84 28 3520 9999

4. Caravelle Saigon

A historic hotel with a contemporary twist, Caravelle Saigon has been a landmark since 1959. Located in the city center, it offers a blend of classic charm and modern amenities. Guests can relax in well-appointed rooms, enjoy the rooftop pool, and dine at the hotel's acclaimed restaurants.

Price Range: $180 - $400 per night

Location: 19-23 Lam Son Square, District 1, Ho Chi Minh City

Contact: +84 28 3823 4999

5. Sheraton Saigon Hotel & Towers

Sheraton Saigon Hotel & Towers offers luxurious accommodations with panoramic views of the city and the Saigon River. The hotel is ideally situated in the heart of the entertainment and business district. It features a rooftop bar, an outdoor pool, and a variety of dining options, ensuring a delightful stay.

Price Range: $200 - $450 per night

Location: District 1, Ho Chi Minh City, 88 Dong Khoi

Contact: +84 28 3827 2828

Travel Tips:

Book Early: Luxury hotels in Ho Chi Minh City are popular, so booking in advance ensures you get the best rates and preferred room types.

Check for Promotions: Many hotels offer special packages that include meals, spa treatments, or city tours.

Explore the Surroundings: Staying in District 1 provides easy access to key attractions like Ben Thanh Market, Notre Dame Cathedral, and the Saigon Opera House.

Use Hotel Concierge Services: The concierge can help arrange local tours, dining reservations, and other activities to enhance your stay.

MID-RANGE HOTELS

1. Silverland Jolie Hotel & Spa

Location: Conveniently situated in District 1, Silverland Jolie Hotel & Spa offers easy access to major attractions such as the Saigon Opera House and Notre Dame Cathedral.

Address: Ben Nghe Ward, District 1, 4D Thi Sach Street, Ho Chi Minh City, Vietnam

Phone Number: +84 28 3829 3266

Price Range: $70 - $120 per night

Tips: Enjoy the rooftop pool with panoramic views of the city and Saigon River. The hotel also offers a daily afternoon tea, which is a great way to relax after a day of exploring.

2. Liberty Central Saigon Citypoint Hotel

Location: Located in the heart of District 1, Liberty Central Saigon Citypoint Hotel is within walking distance to Ben Thanh Market and the War Remnants Museum.

Address: 59 - 61 Pasteur Street, Ben Nghe Ward, District 1, Ho Chi Minh City, Vietnam

Phone Number: +84 28 3822 5678

Price Range: $80 - $130 per night

Tips: Take advantage of the hotel's rooftop bar and infinity pool for a relaxing evening with a great view. The hotel also has a cinema, perfect for unwinding after a day of sightseeing.

3. Alagon Zen Hotel & Spa

Location: Situated near the famous Ben Thanh Market, Alagon Zen Hotel & Spa offers a central location with easy access to many of the city's attractions.

Address: 46 Thu Khoa Huan Street, Ben Thanh Ward, District 1, Ho Chi Minh City, Vietnam

Phone Number: +84 28 3827 2738

Price Range: $60 - $110 per night

Tips: Don't miss out on the hotel's spa services, which provide a perfect way to relax after a busy day. The rooftop garden and Jacuzzi are also excellent spots to unwind.

4. The Myst Dong Khoi

Location: Nestled in the vibrant Dong Khoi area, The Myst Dong Khoi is surrounded by shops, restaurants, and historic landmarks.

Address: 6-8 Ho Huan Nghiep Street, Ben Nghe Ward, District 1, Ho Chi Minh City, Vietnam

Phone Number: +84 28 3520 3040

Price Range: $90 - $150 per night

Tips: Enjoy the unique and artistic design of the hotel, which blends modern comfort with traditional Vietnamese elements. The rooftop pool offers stunning views of the Saigon River.

5. Norfolk Hotel Saigon

Location: Located in the central business district, Norfolk Hotel Saigon is close to major attractions like the Reunification Palace and Saigon Notre-Dame Basilica.

Address: 117 Le Thanh Ton Street, Ben Nghe Ward, District 1, Ho Chi Minh City, Vietnam

Phone Number: +84 28 3829 5368

Price Range: $70 - $120 per night

Tips: The hotel's restaurant offers delicious Vietnamese and international cuisine. Guests can also enjoy the sauna and fitness center, perfect for staying active during your trip.

BUDGET HOSTELS AND GUESTHOUSES

1. The Common Room Project

Located in the heart of District 5, The Common Room Project is more than just a place to sleep. It's a space where you can connect with fellow travelers, enjoy communal dinners, and even take part in movie nights. The stylish, clean dormitories and private rooms come with comfortable beds and modern facilities. Prices for dormitory beds start at around $10 per night, while private rooms can go up to $35.

Address: 80/8 Nguyen Trai, District 5, Ho Chi Minh City

Phone: +84 28 6273 6808

2. Hideout Hostel Saigon

Hideout Hostel Saigon is known for its lively atmosphere and excellent social events, perfect for solo travelers looking to make new friends. Situated in District 1, it provides easy access to the city's top attractions. The hostel offers free breakfast, nightly free beer, and various tours. Dormitory beds are priced from $8, making them a top choice for budget travelers.

Address: District 1, Ho Chi Minh City, 281 Pham Ngu Lao

Phone: +84 28 3920 7654

3. The Like Hostel & Cafe

This charming hostel is located in District 1 and features both dormitory beds and private rooms. The Like Hostel & Cafe boasts a cozy atmosphere with its coffee shop on the premises. Guests can enjoy a complimentary breakfast and use the hostel's communal kitchen. Prices start at $6 for dorm beds and around $25 for private rooms.

Address: 150/37 Nguyen Trai, Ben Thanh Ward, District 1, Ho Chi Minh City

Phone: +84 90 259 6534

4. Town House 50

Town House 50 offers a blend of modern comfort and traditional Vietnamese charm. Located in District 1, it is just a short walk from the Ben Thanh Market. The guesthouse features clean, air-conditioned rooms and a friendly staff ready to assist with travel plans. Dormitory beds are available from $9, while private rooms start at $30.

Address: 50E Bui Thi Xuan, District 1, Ho Chi Minh City

Phone: +84 28 3926 0099

5. Suite Backpackers Inn

Suite Backpackers Inn is a cozy hostel located in the bustling backpacker area of District 1. It offers both dormitory and private rooms with free breakfast, Wi-Fi, and friendly service. The hostel organizes various activities, making it easy to meet other travelers. Dormitory beds start at $7, and private rooms are available from $20.

Address: 227 De Tham, Pham Ngu Lao Ward, District 1, Ho Chi Minh City

Phone: +84 28 3837 9945

UNIQUE STAYS (BOUTIQUE HOTELS, HOMESTAYS)

1. The Myst Dong Khoi

Located in the heart of District 1, The Myst Dong Khoi is a perfect blend of contemporary design and traditional Vietnamese elements. This boutique hotel stands out with its artistic decor, lush greenery, and rooftop pool offering panoramic views of the city.

Tips:

Request a room with a balcony to enjoy the cityscape.

Don't miss the afternoon tea served in the lobby.

Price: From $120 per night

Location: 6-8 Ho Huan Nghiep, District 1, Ho Chi Minh City

Phone: +84 28 3520 3040

2. Villa Song Saigon

Villa Song Saigon offers a serene escape along the banks of the Saigon River. This boutique hotel features elegant rooms, a tranquil garden, and an outdoor pool. The on-site restaurant serves delicious international cuisine with a stunning river view.

Tips:

Take advantage of the complimentary boat transfer to the city center.

Enjoy a sunset cocktail by the river.

Price: From $150 per night

Location: 197/2 Nguyen Van Huong, Thao Dien Ward, District 2, Ho Chi Minh City

Phone: +84 28 3744 6090

3. The Alcove Library Hotel

For book lovers, The Alcove Library Hotel is a hidden gem. Located in Phu Nhuan District, this hotel features a cozy library filled with books and comfortable reading nooks. The rooms are stylish and modern, providing a quiet retreat from the bustling city.

Tips:

Spend some time in the library for a relaxing read.

Try the breakfast at Bookmark, the hotel's rooftop restaurant.

Price: From $80 per night

Location: 133A Nguyen Dinh Chinh, Ward 8, Phu Nhuan District, Ho Chi Minh City

Phone: +84 28 6256 9966

4. Maison De Camille Boutique Hotel

Maison De Camille is a charming boutique hotel situated in Binh Thanh District. Every room has a distinct design that combines modern and old elements. The hotel offers a homely atmosphere with excellent service, making it a great choice for travelers seeking comfort and convenience.

Tips:

Ask for local dining recommendations from the friendly staff.

Enjoy a leisurely breakfast on the terrace.

Price: From $70 per night

Location: 174/21 Dien Bien Phu, Ward 17, Binh Thanh District, Ho Chi Minh City

Phone: +84 28 3512 3540

5. Lief Pulo Saigon

Lief Pulo Saigon provides a colorful and artistic stay in the city. Located in Binh Thanh District, this boutique hotel features spacious rooms with vibrant decor and thoughtful amenities. The rooftop bar is a perfect spot to unwind with a drink.

Tips:

Opt for a suite with a balcony for extra space and views.

Make use of the free bicycles to explore the neighborhood.

Price: From $60 per night

Location: 30/57B Nguyen Cuu Van, Ward 17, Binh Thanh District, Ho Chi Minh City

Phone: +84 28 3514 0999

CHAPTER 3

NAVIGATING THE CITY

PUBLIC TRANSPORTATION (BUSES, METRO)

Buses

Buses are the backbone of Ho Chi Minh City's public transit system. They connect many regions of the city, such as prominent tourist attractions, shopping districts, and residential communities. The buses are an inexpensive option, with fares often ranging from 5,000 to 10,000 VND (about 20 to 40 cents). Tickets can be purchased directly from the driver or at bus terminals.

Several main roads are especially helpful for visitors:

Route 1 connects Ben Thanh Market and Cho Lon, going through key business districts and cultural attractions.

Route 35 is ideal for touring, and stopping at destinations such as the War Remnants Museum, Notre-Dame Cathedral, and Reunification Palace.

Route 152: A handy choice for travelers to and from Tan Son Nhat International Airport, with direct connectivity to the city center.

Buses in Ho Chi Minh City are typically safe and clean, though they can become crowded during peak hours. To efficiently navigate the routes and schedules, keep a map or a transportation app nearby.

Metro

Ho Chi Minh City's metro system is still in progress, but when completed, it promises to transform urban transportation. Line 1, the metro's initial line, is slated to operate soon, connecting Ben Thanh Market and Suoi Tien Park in District 9. This line will greatly minimize travel time between the city center and the eastern suburbs.

The metro will provide a speedier and more pleasant alternative to buses, particularly for longer trips. It is built to meet worldwide standards, with contemporary trains, air-conditioned coaches, and easy-to-use stops. When fully operational, the metro will have many lines that serve all important areas, making it easier for inhabitants and visitors to get around the city.

Practical Tips

Plan: Use online maps and transit applications to plot your trips. Knowing the schedules and stops in advance will help you save time and stress.

Avoid Peak Hours: To avoid the busiest times on buses, travel outside of rush hours (7-9 AM and 5-7 PM).

Stay alert: While public transportation is generally safe, it is always advisable to keep a watch on your valuables, particularly in congested locations.

Learn basic phrases: A few Vietnamese phrases can be useful when asking for directions or purchasing tickets.

TAXIS AND RIDE-SHARING SERVICES

Taxis in Ho Chi Minh City

Taxis are a common sight on the streets of Ho Chi Minh City. They offer a comfortable and reliable way to travel, whether you're heading to a popular tourist spot, a restaurant, or just exploring different neighborhoods. Well-known cab services are Vinasun and Mai Linh. These companies are known for their professionalism and adherence to meter usage, ensuring fair pricing.

When hailing a taxi, look for those with the company logo and a working meter. It's advisable to avoid unmarked taxis as they might overcharge or take longer routes. The base fare is reasonable, and fares increase at a steady rate per kilometer, making it easy to keep track of your travel costs.

Ride-Sharing Services

In recent years, ride-sharing services like Grab have become incredibly popular in Ho Chi Minh City. These services are accessible through mobile apps, offering a convenient alternative to traditional taxis. With Grab, you can easily book a ride from your smartphone, track your driver's arrival, and even pay through the app, eliminating the need for cash.

Ride-sharing services are particularly useful for their transparent pricing, which is calculated upfront before you confirm your ride. This feature helps you avoid any surprises and allows you to choose from different vehicle options based on your budget and preference. Additionally, the ability to leave reviews helps maintain a high standard of service among drivers.

Tips for Using Taxis and Ride-Sharing Services

Download the Necessary Apps: If you plan to use ride-sharing services, ensure you download the necessary apps before your trip. This will save you time and help you get accustomed to the interface.

Have Small Change Ready: For taxi rides, having small changes can be helpful, especially if the driver doesn't have enough change for larger bills.

Check Your Destination: Whether you're in a taxi or a ride-share, double-check that the driver knows your destination. Showing the address or location on a map can prevent misunderstandings.

Use Hotel Services: If you're unsure about hailing a taxi on the street, ask your hotel to call one for you. This ensures you get a reputable service.

Stay Aware of Traffic Conditions: Ho Chi Minh City is known for its bustling traffic. Allow extra time for your trips, especially during peak hours.

RENTING MOTORBIKES AND BICYCLES

Rent a Motorbike

Many people and tourists alike use motorcycles as their primary means of transportation. They make it easy for you to get to places that may be harder to get to by automobile and to maneuver the busy roadways. A large range of motorbikes, from scooters to more powerful models, are available for rent from several stores located throughout the city.

Verify that your driver's license is valid before renting. Even while some rental companies might not verify, it's crucial for both legal compliance and your safety. Depending on the bike's make and model, rental prices can range from $5 to $10 per day, making them generally reasonable. It's best to give the motorcycle a full inspection before using it. Inspect the tires, fuel level, brakes, and lights. Helmets are provided by many stores and are legally required.

Rental Bicycles

Bicycles are a great option for people who want to travel more slowly and sustainably. You can take your time and enjoy the sights, sounds, and fragrances of Ho Chi Minh City while cycling throughout the city. Bicycles can be rented from a variety of places, including certain hotels and guesthouses.

The cost to hire a bicycle is normally $2 to $5 per day. Just like with motorcycles, make sure the bicycle is in good working order before riding. Verify the tire pressure, gears, and brakes. For your protection, wearing a helmet is highly advised.

Safety Advice

Safety should be your primary concern while selecting a vehicle, be it a bicycle or a motorbike. It can be quite difficult to navigate the traffic in Ho Chi Minh City, particularly for first-time tourists. The tips below will assist you in staying secure:

Keep Your Eyes Open: The traffic is chaotic and hectic. Keep an eye out for other cars and stay conscious of your surroundings at all times.

Observe traffic laws: Observe traffic signals and drive on the right side of the road. At intersections, exercise caution.

Use Maps: To navigate, use a map app or GPS. This will assist you in locating the best routes and preventing lostness.

Safeguard Your Items: Store your valuables somewhere safe and hidden to deter theft. Make use of a safe bag or a backpack.

Drink plenty of water and use sun protection since the weather can get rather hot and muggy. To stay hydrated, bring water and wear a hat, sunglasses, and sunscreen.

Locations to Go

You may travel the city and discover a range of sights on your bike or motorcycle. For a look into Vietnam's past, visit the famous Notre Dame Cathedral Basilica, the War Remnants Museum, and the old Saigon Central Post Office. Enjoy the lively Ben Thanh Market, where you can sample delectable street cuisine and learn about the native way of life.

Take a bike ride to the Botanical Gardens or Tao Dan Park for a tranquil escape. Consider taking a lengthier trip to the Cu Chi Tunnels, which are roughly 70 kilometers outside the city center, if you're up for it. An intriguing glimpse into the subterranean network utilized in the Vietnam War is provided by these tunnels.

WALKING TOURS

Begin your journey at the city's core, Ben Thanh Market. This lively marketplace is a sensory delight, with sellers offering everything from fresh food to artisan trinkets. Take your time wandering among the vendors, trying local specialties and even picking up some souvenirs from your journey.

From Ben Thanh Market, proceed to the Notre-Dame Cathedral Basilica of Saigon. This lovely red-brick church, constructed by French immigrants in the nineteenth century, is an excellent example of neo-Romanesque architecture. Nearby, you'll find

Gustave Eiffel's Saigon Central Post Office. This old structure is still in use, and its majestic interior is worth seeing.

As you continue your walk, head towards the Reunification Palace. This famous structure played a significant role in Vietnamese history, serving as the location of the Vietnam War's end in 1975. The palace is now a museum, with guided tours offered to help visitors comprehend its historical significance.

The War Remnants Museum is located a short walk from the Reunification Palace. This museum provides a somber look into the Vietnam War through the eyes of the Vietnamese people. The exhibits feature images, military equipment, and personal accounts that provide a thorough understanding of the struggle and its influence on the country.

After visiting the museum, walk down Dong Khoi Street, one of Ho Chi Minh City's most famous thoroughfares. This bustling boulevard is dotted with stores, cafés, and colonial-era structures. It's a nice area to relax, have a coffee, and people-watch.

Visit the Jade Emperor Pagoda to experience local spirituality. This atmospheric temple honors different Taoist gods and is decorated with beautiful carvings, statues, and incense. It's a calm refuge from the city's hustle and bustle, as well as an insight into the people's spiritual lives.

CHAPTER 4

TOP ATTRACTIONS

HISTORICAL SITES (REUNIFICATION PALACE, WAR REMNANTS MUSEUM)

Reunification Palace

The Reunification Palace, also known as the Independence Palace, is located in the middle of the city and serves as a symbol of Vietnam's transition from conflict to peace. This landmark is more than just an architectural masterpiece; it is also a historical symbol of the end of the Vietnam War. During the war, the Palace served as the residence of South Vietnam's President and witnessed the pivotal moment when a North Vietnamese tank broke through its gates on April 30, 1975, signifying Saigon's capitulation.

Visitors can visit the well-preserved chambers, such as the president's office, the war room, and the telecommunications center, which reflect the era's décor and technological developments. The basement, a complex of tunnels and battle rooms, is a striking reminder of the strategic activities carried out during the war. Walking around the spacious gardens, with their quiet mood, one might reflect on the juxtaposition between the Palace's peaceful surroundings and its historical importance.

War Remnant Museum

The War Remnants Museum, located near the Reunification Palace, offers a candid look at the effects of the Vietnam War. The museum, which opened to the public in 1975, has since become one of the city's most popular tourist destinations, attracting both international and local visitors.

The museum's exhibits are intelligently arranged to portray the war's terrible realities and long-term consequences. The courtyard houses military equipment such as tanks, aircraft, and bombs, providing a concrete link to the past. The exhibitions are organized into thematic rooms that focus on different parts of the war, such as the "Historical Truths" gallery, which provides context through images, papers, and relics.

One of the most moving pieces is the "Agent Orange Aftermath" display, which depicts the devastating effects of chemical warfare on the environment and human health. Photographs, personal testimonies, and elaborate exhibits provide a very touching experience that encourages thought on the war's human cost.

Visiting Tips:

Visitors should prepare to spend a few hours at each location to truly understand the amount of history and knowledge provided. The Reunification Palace provides guided tours in a variety of languages, offering significant insights and historical context. At the War Remnants Museum, reading through the extensive explanations and personal accounts enhances the overall experience.

Both locations are easily accessible via public transportation or a short walk if you are staying in the central district. Early morning or late afternoon visits can help you avoid the daytime heat and throng, resulting in a more pleasant and thoughtful tour.

RELIGIOUS SITES (NOTRE-DAME CATHEDRAL BASILICA, JADE EMPEROR PAGODA)

Notre Dame Cathedral Basilica, located in the middle of the city, is a magnificent emblem of French colonial influence in Vietnam. This spectacular edifice, built between 1877 and 1880, was entirely made of materials imported from France. The red bricks, imported from Toulouse, have retained their original color, giving the church a distinguishing aspect.

Its twin bell towers, each standing over 190 feet tall, dominate the skyline and serve as a conspicuous landmark. The interior, however basic when compared to European cathedrals, radiates a tranquil and solemn aura. Stained glass windows, painstakingly rebuilt following wartime damage, create vivid patterns of light across the oak pews, creating a peaceful environment for thought and prayer.

Just a short distance from downtown, the Jade Emperor Pagoda provides a unique spiritual experience. This Taoist temple, built in 1909 by the city's Cantonese community, is devoted to the Jade Emperor, Taoism's greatest god. The pagoda is a sensory feast, with exquisite carvings, statues of numerous deities, and the pleasant aroma of incense filling the air.

The entryway is guarded by statues of strong warriors, which represent protection from evil spirits. Inside, the main hall features a statue of the Jade Emperor surrounded by various deities and mythical beings. The beautiful woodwork and richly painted altars demonstrate the temple builders' skill and commitment. A tiny pond at the back of the temple is filled with turtles, which are regarded as emblems of longevity, contributing to the pagoda's tranquil atmosphere.

MODERN LANDMARKS (BITEXCO FINANCIAL TOWER, LANDMARK 81)

The Bitexco Financial Tower is an outstanding tower that has become linked with the city's fast modernization. This architectural masterpiece, standing at 262.5 meters tall, was finished in 2010 and is notable for its unusual helipad that protrudes from the 52nd level. The design of the skyscraper was inspired by Vietnam's national flower, the lotus, reflecting the country's growth and prosperity.

Visitors to the Bitexco Financial Tower can enjoy a panoramic view of Ho Chi Minh City from the Saigon Skydeck on the 49th floor. The observation deck offers a 360-degree perspective, providing a fantastic opportunity to admire the city's expansive landscape and busy canals. For those wishing to unwind with a drink while taking in the view, EON51, a café and restaurant located on the top floors, offers a magnificent environment and a menu filled with local and foreign food.

Another spectacular structure that dominates the city's skyline is Landmark 81. Completed in 2018, this skyscraper stands at 461.2

meters, making it Vietnam's tallest building. Landmark 81 is part of the Vinhomes Central Park urban area and has a sleek, modern style that embodies the city's forward-thinking character.

Landmark 81 is more than just a towering skyscraper; it's a hive of activity and elegance. The bottom floors are home to a high-end shopping center, where visitors may discover a variety of local and worldwide brands. For those seeking adventure, the Landmark 81 SkyView on the 79th to 81st floors provides thrilling experiences such as virtual reality games and an ice-skating rink. The observation deck here also affords a spectacular perspective of the city, particularly beautiful around nightfall when the city lights begin to twinkle.

For a remarkable dining experience, the skyscraper has numerous upmarket restaurants, including a steakhouse and a Japanese restaurant, both delivering exquisite meals with a side of stunning views. Additionally, the Vinpearl Luxury Hotel occupies the upper levels, providing guests with excellent accommodations and services.

CULTURAL SITES (HO CHI MINH CITY MUSEUM, FINE ARTS MUSEUM)

The Ho Chi Minh City Museum is a must-see for anyone interested in the city's history. The museum, housed in a great French colonial structure, is a historical piece. Its design, with magnificent balconies and wide hallways, sets the setting for the antiquities inside.

As you walk through the exhibitions, you'll see a broad collection ranging from ancient relics to things from the Vietnam War. Archaeology, trade, culture, and the revolutionary struggle are all represented in separate rooms. The museum tells a detailed story about how Ho Chi Minh City evolved over the years, making it an interesting spot to spend a few hours.

The Fine Arts Museum, located near the Ho Chi Minh City Museum, is another must-see for cultural fans. This museum is housed in a lovely colonial-era edifice that exemplifies the architectural style of the time. Inside, you'll find an astonishing collection of artworks that showcase the originality and talent of Vietnamese artists.

The collection contains traditional paintings, modern art, sculptures, and ceramics. Each item tells a tale, offering an insight into the cultural and creative legacy of Vietnam. The museum's arrangement, divided across three floors, allows visitors to appreciate both the historical and present contributions to the arts.

It's a calm space where one may appreciate the richness and diversity of Vietnamese art.

CHAPTER 5

NEIGHBORHOODS TO EXPLORE

DISTRICT 1: THE HEART OF THE CITY

Begin your adventure at Ben Thanh Market, a vibrant center of commerce and social interaction. Fresh fruit, street food, and one-of-a-kind souvenirs are all available here. The aroma of Vietnamese coffee blends with the scent of freshly cooked items in the market, creating a sensory feast.

A short stroll from the market leads to the Saigon Notre-Dame Basilica, the city's distinctive landmark. This gorgeous cathedral, erected during the French colonial period, displays beautiful neo-Romanesque design and provides a tranquil respite from the city's hustle and bustle.

Next, go to the Saigon Central Post Office, an architectural marvel created by Gustave Eiffel. Step inside to see the enormous interior and well-preserved decorations, and consider sending a postcard home.

The War Remnants Museum offers a more in-depth look at the city's past. The displays here provide a dramatic look into the Vietnam War from the Vietnamese perspective, serving as a somber reminder of the past.

Tao Dan Park is an excellent choice for anyone looking for some green space. It's a terrific area to unwind, people-watch, or join residents for their morning tai chi sessions. The park's peaceful environment offers a nice contrast to the city's hectic streets.

Dong Khoi Street, a lively street, is another District 1 feature. This historic boulevard is lined with high-end stores, art galleries, and cafes, providing a mix of old and new. It's a terrific spot to walk, shop, and absorb the city's global atmosphere.

For a taste of luxury, go to the Rex Hotel Rooftop Bar. This landmark location provides panoramic views of the city as well as a wide range of beverages. It's the ideal spot to unwind following a full day of sightseeing.

Finally, make sure to see the Bitexco Financial Tower. The Skydeck on the 49th floor offers amazing views of the city skyline and the Saigon River. It's the ideal way to wrap out your day in District 1, taking in the breathtaking view as the city lights up at night.

DISTRICT 3: COLONIAL ARCHITECTURE AND LOCAL VIBES

As you travel around District 3, you'll note the French colonial influence in the architecture. The streets are lined with elegant buildings that feature shuttered windows, wrought-iron balconies, and majestic facades. One of the most noteworthy examples is the Jade Emperor Pagoda, a magnificent pagoda constructed in the early 1900s. This architectural marvel is embellished with beautiful carvings and statues, offering a peaceful respite amidst the metropolitan chaos.

Another must-visit is the Tan Dinh Church, widely referred to as the "Pink Church" because of its distinctive pink facade. This Roman Catholic Church, constructed in the late nineteenth century, is an excellent blend of Gothic and Renaissance architectural styles. Its towering spires and elaborate interior make it an intriguing destination for history and architecture buffs.

District 3 is also home to many neighborhood markets and street food sellers. These lively eateries provide a variety of classic Vietnamese meals. Vietnamese cuisine, including phở and bánh mì, as well as fresh spring rolls, is a delicious taste of the country's culinary heritage. These markets' sights, sounds, and smells provide tourists with an authentic experience that connects them to the city's daily life.

The area's tree-lined streets and parks create a beautiful setting for a stroll. Le Van Tam Park is a popular green spot where locals come for fitness, socializing, and leisure. The park's shaded trails and open spaces provide a tranquil respite from the bustling streets.

Art and culture fans will like District 3's numerous galleries and cultural centers. These locations exhibit contemporary Vietnamese art and hold a variety of cultural events, providing insight into the country's creative environment. The environment is vibrant and pleasant, reflecting the district's dynamic nature.

District 3 offers a variety of boutiques and businesses selling everything from homemade crafts to contemporary apparel. These boutiques promote local workmanship and design, offering one-of-a-kind souvenirs and gifts.

Staying in District 3 provides a new viewpoint on Ho Chi Minh City. While not as touristy as District 1, its appeal stems from its realism and the daily lives of its citizens. Accommodations range from boutique hotels to lovely guesthouses, providing a comfortable stay with a personal touch.

DISTRICT 5: CHOLON (CHINATOWN)

Cholon's streets are packed with activity, ranging from lively markets to traditional Chinese temples. One of the attractions is the Binh Tay Market, a well-known site where you can find a variety of things. This market offers an authentic view of Cholon's daily life, with fresh food and spices as well as unusual gifts. The market's architecture is a lovely blend of French and Chinese designs, which adds to its appeal.

Cholon's temples are another prominent attraction. The Thien Hau Temple, dedicated to the Lady of the Sea, is especially significant. This temple, created by the Chinese minority, is decorated with beautiful carvings and figures, creating a peaceful environment. The burning incense coils and sandalwood aroma enhance the spiritual experience, creating a tranquil escape from the city's rush and bustle.

Cholon is also known for its culinary pleasures. The area has a variety of food vendors and restaurants serving wonderful Chinese and Vietnamese cuisine. Cholon's delicacies, which range from dim sum and noodle soups to freshly prepared dumplings, would gratify any foodie. Don't pass up trying a bowl of pho or a plate of delectable spring rolls.

Walking through the streets of Cholon, you'll come across a unique blend of old and new. Traditional medical shops coexist with modern establishments, while street sellers offer anything from herbs to technology. The lively street life and friendly inhabitants enhance the neighborhood's appeal.

Another notable location is the Quan Am Pagoda, a stunning pagoda dedicated to the Goddess of Mercy. This temple, with its intricate decorations and serene gardens, is an excellent site to learn about Chinese religious customs while also finding peace.

Cholon's preserved architecture and cultural assets provide a look into the past for historians. The region has a long history, dating back to the 18th century when Chinese immigrants lived there. Today, it is an important cultural hub that reflects the customs and lifestyles of its residents.

DISTRICT 7: MODERN URBAN LIVING

District 7, located just a short drive from the city center, and provides a welcome respite from the hectic pace of other areas in Ho Chi Minh City. This district is distinguished by its well-planned infrastructure, spacious boulevards, and clean, ordered streets. It provides a peaceful retreat with a variety of attractions and amenities tailored to a modern lifestyle.

The Crescent Mall, a premier shopping destination with a diverse selection of foreign and local brands, is one of District 7's attractions. This sophisticated shopping center serves as both a shopping destination and a social hub where people may gather for food, entertainment, and leisure activities. Crescent Mall offers a comprehensive experience for guests, with a variety of restaurants providing global cuisines, coffee shops, and a cutting-edge theater.

The beautiful Crescent Lake and its surrounding park are adjacent to Crescent Mall. This location is ideal for taking a stroll, jogging, or simply enjoying the peaceful surroundings. The lake is a popular destination for both daytime and evening activities, providing a lovely backdrop with its well-planted gardens and tranquil waters.

District 7 is well noted for its diversified food scene. From high-end restaurants to intimate cafes and street food vendors, there is something for everyone's taste. The district is particularly well-known for its diverse international dining options, which represent the local expatriate community. Whether you crave Japanese sushi, Korean BBQ, Italian pasta, or authentic Vietnamese pho, District 7 has it all.

For individuals interested in culture and education, the Saigon Exhibition and Convention Center (SECC) holds several international events, trade exhibits, and exhibitions each year. It is an important arena that brings together professionals from diverse businesses, contributing to the district's thriving economic environment.

District 7 takes pride in its educational institutions, which include various foreign schools and colleges that provide high-quality education. This makes it a popular residential location for both expatriates and locals looking for a sophisticated lifestyle with access to outstanding educational opportunities.

The district's residential areas further demonstrate its modernism and comfort. Phu My Hung, a notable urban district in District 7, is known for its well-planned residential complexes, green areas, and community amenities. It offers a calm and secure living environment, making it an excellent choice for families and professionals.

CHAPTER 6

CULINARY EXPERIENCES

STREET FOOD HIGHLIGHTS

Bánh Mì

A trip to Ho Chi Minh City isn't complete without trying bánh mì. This Vietnamese sandwich is the ideal combination of French and Vietnamese culinary traditions. It normally consists of a crispy baguette filled with a variety of meats, pâté, pickled vegetables, fresh herbs, and chile. Each bite contains a delicious combination of flavors and textures, making it a popular street dish.

Phở

Phở, a fragrant noodle soup, is also a well-known cuisine worldwide. Phở is typically served hot with fresh herbs, lime, and chile, and can be cooked with beef or chicken. The rich, aromatic soup is cooked for hours, producing a warm and savory dinner suitable for any time of day.

Gỏi Cuốn (spring rolls)

Fresh spring rolls, also known as gỏi cuốn, are an excellent lighter option. These rolls are filled with shrimp, pork, vermicelli noodles, and a variety of fresh herbs, all wrapped in rice paper. They are usually served with a side of peanut dipping sauce, which provides a delightful savory flavor to every bite.

Bánh xèo

Bánh xèo, often known as Vietnamese pancakes, are crispy, savory crepes prepared from rice flour and coconut milk, and filled with shrimp, pork, and bean sprouts. The pancakes are folded in half and served with a side of fresh herbs and lettuce, which are wrapped around the pancakes before being dipped in a tangy fish sauce.

Hu Tiêu

Hu Tieu is a versatile noodle meal that can be eaten as a soup or dry with a side of broth. This meal comprises chewy noodles topped with pork, shrimp, and quail eggs. Each vendor adds their twist to hu tieu, making it a dish worth eating from various stands.

Bột Chiên

Bột chiên, a popular snack among locals, is formed with rice flour cakes fried until crispy and topped with eggs. It is usually served with a side of pickled papaya and a sour soy-based dipping sauce. This savory dish is especially popular in the evenings, with many young people enjoying it as a late-night snack.

Che

Che provides a delicious ending to your street food experience. Che is a Vietnamese sweet soup or pudding that comes in a variety of flavors, including beans, fruit, coconut milk, and jellies. It's a welcome relief in the hot and humid weather of Ho Chi Minh City.

MUST-TRY DISHES (PHO, BANH MI, GOI CUON)

Pho, a typical Vietnamese noodle soup, is a culinary delight. This dish is made of a fragrant broth cooked for hours with cattle bones, herbs, and spices. Pho is typically served with beef or chicken and garnished with fresh herbs, lime wedges, bean sprouts, and chili slices. This mix of ingredients results in a flavor harmony that is both cozy and refreshing. Many street vendors and small cafes in Ho Chi Minh City serve their versions of this famous dish, which has become a Vietnamese culinary staple.

Banh mi, another must-try, is a Vietnamese sandwich that expertly combines French and Vietnamese culinary traditions. It begins with a crispy baguette, a vestige of French colonial influence, and is then filled with a variety of fillings.

Grilled pork, pate, pickled vegetables, fresh cilantro, and a dab of chili sauce are popular fillings. The crunchy bread contrasts with the savory, spicy, and sour ingredients, resulting in a pleasant flavor experience. As you explore the city, you'll come across various street sellers making these delectable sandwiches, each with their unique touch.

Goi cuon, often known as fresh spring rolls, is a lighter but tasty alternative. These rolls are constructed with rice paper with a mixture of shrimp, pork, fresh herbs, vermicelli noodles, and lettuce. Goi cuon, which is typically served with a side of hoisin or peanut sauce for dipping, is a refreshing and healthful option for a quick snack or light lunch. These rolls are popular among both locals and visitors due to their fresh ingredients and burst of flavors with each bite.

BEST RESTAURANTS AND EATERIES

The Refinery

Located in a charming colonial courtyard, The Refinery is a popular spot for both locals and tourists. The menu features a mix of French and Vietnamese dishes, all made with fresh, high-quality ingredients. It's a must-visit because of the wonderful service and welcoming ambiance.

Location: 74 Hai Ba Trung, Ben Nghe Ward, District 1, Ho Chi Minh City

Phone: +84 28 3823 0509

Quan An Ngon

Quan An Ngon is renowned for its authentic Vietnamese cuisine. Set in a beautiful villa, the restaurant offers a wide variety of dishes from different regions of Vietnam. The open kitchen allows diners to watch as their food is prepared, adding to the overall experience.

Location: 160 Pasteur, Ben Nghe Ward, District 1, Ho Chi Minh City

Phone: +84 28 3827 9666

Cuc Gach Quan

Cuc Gach Quan provides a rustic dining experience with a menu that emphasizes organic and healthy options. The restaurant is housed in a traditional Vietnamese home, and the decor reflects a blend of old and new. The home-style cooking and friendly service make it a favorite among those looking for a more authentic meal.

Location: Tan Dinh Ward, District 1, 10 Dang Tat, Ho Chi Minh City

Phone: +84 28 3848 0144

Pizza 4P's

If you're craving pizza, Pizza 4P's is the place to go. This Japanese-owned restaurant offers some of the best pizzas in the city, with a unique twist. The ingredients are sourced locally and internationally, ensuring top-notch quality. The atmosphere is relaxed, making it perfect for a casual meal.

Location: District 1, Ho Chi Minh City, 8/15 Le Thanh Ton, Ben Nghe Ward

Phone: +84 28 3622 0500

Secret Garden

Hidden away in a rooftop location, Secret Garden offers a peaceful escape from the city's hustle and bustle. The menu features traditional Vietnamese dishes, all prepared with a modern touch. The charming setting and delicious food make it a great spot for a quiet dinner.

Location: 158 Pasteur, Ben Nghe Ward, District 1, Ho Chi Minh City

Phone: +84 90 990 46 21

Hum Vegetarian

For vegetarians and vegans, Hum Vegetarian is a top choice. The restaurant serves creative and beautifully presented dishes in a tranquil setting. The focus on fresh, locally sourced ingredients ensures that every meal is both healthy and delicious.

Location: 32 Vo Van Tan, Ward 6, District 3, Ho Chi Minh City

Phone: +84 28 3930 3819

Propaganda Bistro

Propaganda Bistro offers a modern take on traditional Vietnamese street food. The vibrant and colorful decor, combined with the creative menu, makes for a memorable dining experience. It's a great place to try classic dishes with a contemporary twist.

Location: 21 Han Thuyen, Ben Nghe Ward, District 1, Ho Chi Minh City

Phone: +84 28 3822 9048

Nha Hang Ngon

Nha Hang Ngon is another excellent option for those looking to explore Vietnamese cuisine. The restaurant features an extensive menu with dishes from all over the country, served in a beautiful setting that blends modern and traditional elements.

Location: 160 Pasteur, Ben Nghe Ward, District 1, Ho Chi Minh City

Phone: +84 28 3827 7131

Noir. Dining in the Dark

For a unique dining experience, Noir. Dining in the Dark is a must-visit. Guests dine in complete darkness, guided by visually impaired waitstaff. The restaurant offers a surprise menu that heightens the senses and provides a deeper appreciation for the flavors and textures of the food.

Location: 178 Hai Ba Trung, Dakao Ward, District 1, Ho Chi Minh City

Phone: +84 28 6263 2525

L'Usine

L'Usine is a trendy cafe and bistro that combines a modern aesthetic with delicious food. The menu includes a mix of Western and Vietnamese dishes, making it a great spot for brunch or a casual meal. The stylish decor and relaxed atmosphere make it a popular hangout.

Location: 70B Le Loi, Ben Nghe Ward, District 1, Ho Chi Minh City

Phone: +84 28 3521 0703

COOKING CLASSES AND FOOD TOURS

Cooking classes in Ho Chi Minh City are a must-try for anybody who enjoys the culinary arts. These seminars offer a hands-on experience in which participants can learn the secrets of traditional Vietnamese cuisine.

Local chefs will walk you through each step, from choosing fresh products at the market to learning the methods required to produce delectable dishes. Pho, spring rolls, and banh xeo are among the most popular foods taught in these seminars. The seminars are often small and intimate, ensuring customized attention and a welcoming environment.

The market tour is one of the most memorable aspects of our cookery classes. You'll go to lively local markets, where the bright colors and unusual scents create a sensory explosion. You'll learn how to choose the best produce, herbs, and spices for Vietnamese cooking. This section of the session not only teaches you about the components, but also gives you an insight into the daily lives of the locals.

Food tours in Ho Chi Minh City provide another fun opportunity to discover the city's gastronomic offerings. These trips take you through the city's streets, lanes, and markets, sampling authentic Vietnamese street food. You'll discover hidden jewels that you wouldn't have found on your own, thanks to informed locals. These trips offer an incredible range of food, from savory soups and noodle dishes to sweet desserts and refreshing drinks.

The Ben Thanh Market is a renowned culinary tour site, with a historic and bustling marketplace where you may try a variety of Vietnamese foods. Another favorite is Nguyen Hue Walking Street, where merchants sell great delicacies in a bustling, open-air environment. As you walk through the streets, you'll have the opportunity to learn about the history and culture that inspired each dish, making the experience both instructive and pleasurable.

Cooking lessons and cuisine excursions in Ho Chi Minh City provide a cultural experience as well as a culinary adventure. You will obtain a greater understanding of Vietnamese food and the traditions that have shaped it. These activities are ideal for lone travelers, couples, and families, providing a unique opportunity to bond over cuisine and make lasting memories.

CHAPTER 7

SHOPPING GUIDE

TRADITIONAL MARKETS (BEN THANH MARKET, BINH TAY MARKET)

Ben Thanh Market, located in the center of District 1, is one of the oldest and most well-known markets in Ho Chi Minh City. This market, which dates back to the early 17th century, has become a municipal emblem. Its distinctive clock tower serves as a welcoming beacon for visitors. The market is a flurry of activity, with sellers offering everything from fresh vegetables, spices, and seafood to clothing, souvenirs, and handmade items.

Walking through Ben Thanh Market's aisles, you'll be greeted by the vivid colors of tropical fruits and vegetables, the aromatic fragrances of local spices, and the bustling sounds of vendors bartering with customers. It's the perfect place to sample some of the city's best street food. The market's various food stalls serve dishes such as pho, banh mi, and fresh spring rolls. The night market, which appears around Ben Thanh after sunset, has a unique ambiance with its selection of street food and souvenir vendors, making it an ideal site to enjoy local nightlife.

In contrast, Binh Tay Market, located in District 6's Chinatown, offers a more traditional and local shopping experience. This market, built by the French in the 1880s, still retains much of its original architecture and beauty. The market is well-known for its wholesale products, which include textiles, home items, and a wide variety of spices and dry foods.

Binh Tay Market is notably notable for its food court, which serves a variety of Vietnamese and Chinese dishes. The market is also an excellent site to see traditional Vietnamese trade in action, as things are frequently sold in bulk and negotiations take place around every corner. The bustling atmosphere, along with the historical location, make Binh Tay an intriguing place to visit.

MODERN MALLS (SAIGON CENTRE, VINCOM CENTER)

Saigon Centre

Located in the heart of District 1, Saigon Centre is a shining example of modern architecture and elegance. This shopping mall has numerous stories and houses a variety of foreign and local brands. Shoppers can visit high-end fashion boutiques, technology retailers, and specialty shops.

Saigon Centre is more than just a retail destination; it's also a culinary wonderland. The mall has a large food court with many restaurants serving cuisines from across the world. Whether you're wanting Japanese sushi, Italian pasta, or traditional Vietnamese cuisine, you'll find something to suit your taste.

The mall was also developed with comfort and convenience in mind. It provides wide lounging areas, free Wi-Fi, and good customer service. The modern design and well-kept facilities make it a great spot to spend an afternoon, whether shopping or simply relaxing.

Vincom Center

Vincom Center is yet another jewel in Ho Chi Minh City's retail sector. The mall is divided into two sections: Vincom Center A and Vincom Center B. They comprise one of the city's major shopping complexes, with a wide range of products and services.

Vincom Center A is built in a colonial-style building, giving historical character to your shopping experience. Inside, you'll find luxury brands, designer apparel, and premium jewelry shops. The exquisite ambiance and high-end offerings attract both locals and tourists.

Vincom Center B, on the other hand, is a more contemporary construction with a diverse assortment of mid-range and high-end brands. This area of the mall also houses a huge supermarket, a variety of electronics businesses, and home decor retailers. The diversity ensures that there is something for everyone, whether they are seeking everyday necessities or a unique present.

Foodies will appreciate the variety of eating options available at Vincom Center. The mall has various cafes, fast-food eateries, and fine-dining establishments. You can take a quick coffee break or eat a leisurely meal with friends and family all within the same building.

Both Saigon Centre and Vincom Center feature regular events and promotions, which add to the thrill of your visit. From seasonal bargains to cultural events, there's always something going on to improve your shopping experience.

Practical information

When planning your visit, it's helpful to know that both malls are conveniently accessible via numerous kinds of transportation. They are centrally positioned, making them easily accessible whether by taxi, bus, or foot. Additionally, both malls provide abundant parking for anyone driving in the city.

Both malls are open from 9 a.m. to 10 p.m., allowing you plenty of time to explore everything they have to offer. If you want a quieter shopping environment, visit during the weekdays, as weekends can be rather busy.

LOCAL BOUTIQUES AND ARTISAN SHOPS

Begin your journey in District 1, the city's thriving hub. L'Usine is a fashionable concept store that blends fashion, art, and a charming café. This store offers a carefully curated variety of clothing, accessories, and home decor from both local and international designers. The beautiful interior and carefully chosen merchandise make it a must-see for anybody interested in discovering the newest in Vietnamese fashion and design.

Duy Tan - Saigon Artisan, a boutique dedicated to traditional Vietnamese workmanship, is located near L'Usine. The shop sells a variety of handmade items, such as lacquerware, silk scarves, and delicate ceramics. Each item offers a tale about Vietnam's diverse cultural heritage, making them ideal keepsakes or gifts.

The Blue T-shirt is a great option for those who care about sustainable fashion. This business specializes in eco-friendly apparel created from natural fibers and organic components. Their designs are basic but exquisite, evoking a modern spin on traditional Vietnamese style. Shopping here not only benefits local artists but also promotes environmentally responsible methods.

District 3 is home to the delightful SoNice, a store that specializes in handmade goods and decor. The shop's pleasant atmosphere and friendly personnel make browsing their one-of-a-kind variety of jewelry, purses, and homewares enjoyable. Many of the objects are created by local artists utilizing ancient processes, guaranteeing that each piece is unique.

Metiseko, a boutique that specializes in beautiful silk clothes and accessories, is another hidden gem in District 3. The store takes pleasure in employing high-quality, environmentally friendly products and traditional craftsmanship. Their designs frequently integrate motifs influenced by Vietnamese culture, resulting in a stunning blend of legacy and current flair.

For a more diverse shopping experience, visit Ben Thanh Market. While the market is well-known for its lively ambiance and a broad selection of goods, it also includes some kiosks owned by local artisans. Hand-embroidered textiles and one-of-a-kind works of art are all available here. It's a terrific place to get a keepsake and support local artisans.

Tucked away in the calmer lanes of District 5, you'll find The Craft House, a store that sells a chosen collection of handmade goods from across Vietnam. From delicate ceramics to vivid prints, the boutique features the best of Vietnamese craftsmanship. The Craft House is committed to fostering local craftsmen and conserving traditional skills, making it an excellent place to find one-of-a-kind, high-quality products.

Finally, don't pass up the opportunity to visit the Saigon Kitsch in District 1. This shop is full of unique goods and retro-inspired decor. Their vibrant collection of posters, postcards, and homewares portrays the whimsical atmosphere of Ho Chi Minh City, making it an enjoyable and unforgettable shopping experience.

SOUVENIRS TO BUY

Handcrafted lacquerware

Lacquerware is a traditional Vietnamese craft that has evolved over generations. These exquisite artifacts, which range from bowls to paintings, are expertly produced and make lovely ornamental pieces. They come in a variety of sizes and patterns, making them ideal for gifts or as a statement piece in your home decor.

Silk Products

Vietnamese silk is renowned for its quality and beauty. In Ho Chi Minh City, you may get beautiful silk scarves, ties, gowns, and other clothing. Vietnamese silk's silky texture and brilliant hues are guaranteed to impress, adding an air of luxury to any wardrobe.

Ao Dai

The Ao Dai, a traditional Vietnamese dress, exudes grace and beauty. Purchasing an Ao Dai is an excellent way to bring home a bit of Vietnamese culture. These dresses are frequently adjusted to fit, ensuring an ideal fit for you. An Ao Dai, whether modern or traditional, is a lasting souvenir.

Vietnamese Coffee

Vietnam is famed for its coffee, especially the rich and aromatic dark roast. In Ho Chi Minh City, you may get high-quality coffee beans to drink at home. Highlands Coffee and Trung Nguyen are two popular possibilities. Don't forget to buy a traditional Vietnamese coffee filter (phin) so you may make your coffee like the locals.

Ceramics and Pottery

The city has a wide selection of wonderfully crafted ceramics and pottery. These objects are often handcrafted and have beautiful designs that reflect Vietnamese culture. From tea sets to beautiful plates, these items are both utilitarian and visually appealing.

Conical Hats (Non-La)

Non-La, the classic Vietnamese conical hat, is a national symbol of Vietnam. These hats are lightweight, sturdy, and offer good sun protection. They are both functional and charming souvenirs that encapsulate the essence of Vietnamese culture.

Hand-embroidered items

Hand-embroidered items such as tablecloths, pillowcases, and clothes make fantastic souvenirs. These goods highlight Vietnamese artisans' delicate stitching talents and are lovely, one-of-a-kind gifts.

Art and Painting

For art lovers, Ho Chi Minh City has a thriving art scene. You can find galleries and businesses that sell original paintings, prints, and other artworks created by local artists. These pieces frequently represent scenes from Vietnamese life and scenery, creating a vibrant and creative souvenir of your visit.

Spices & Sauces

Bring home the aromas of Vietnam with a variety of local spices and sauces. Popular options include fish sauce, chili sauce, and different spice blends found in Vietnamese cuisine. These culinary souvenirs will enable you to reproduce the delectable foods you sampled during your visit.

Traditional Musical Instruments

If you enjoy music, consider getting a traditional Vietnamese instrument. Other options include the dan bau (monochord), dan tranh (zither), and other unique instruments. These things are not only gorgeous but also provide a unique method to learn about Vietnamese music and culture.

CHAPTER 8

NIGHTLIFE AND ENTERTAINMENT

BARS AND PUBS

1. The Gin House

Location: 28/3A Tôn Thất Tùng, Phạm Ngũ Lão, District 1

Phone Number: +84 28 6656 8899

The Gin House is a cozy bar that specializes in gin-based cocktails. With its relaxed atmosphere and impressive selection of gins from around the world, it's the perfect spot for a quiet night out.

2. Rogue Saigon

Location: 13 Pasteur, District 1

Phone Number: +84 28 3915 3277

Rogue Saigon offers a rooftop bar experience with a wide range of craft beers. Enjoy your drink with a panoramic view of the city skyline.

3. Broma: Not a Bar

Location: 41 Nguyễn Huệ, Bến Nghé, District 1

Phone Number: +84 90 229 19 77

Broma: Not a Bar is known for its lively ambiance and great music. This rooftop bar provides a fun setting to enjoy cocktails and craft beers with friends.

4. The Racha Room

Location: 12-14 Mạc Thị Bưởi, District 1

Phone Number: +84 28 3823 0509

The Racha Room combines great food with a fantastic bar. Known for its modern Thai cuisine and creative cocktails, this bar is perfect for a night out with delicious bites and drinks.

5. Saigon Saigon Rooftop Bar

Location: 19 Lam Son Square, District 1

Phone Number: +84 28 3823 4999

Located on the rooftop of the Caravelle Hotel, Saigon Saigon Rooftop Bar offers a stunning view of the city. This iconic bar is a perfect spot for both tourists and locals to enjoy a sophisticated evening.

6. Layla - Eatery & Bar

Location: 63 Đông Du, Bến Nghé, District 1

Phone Number: +84 28 3827 2279

Layla - Eatery & Bar is a stylish venue that offers a wide range of cocktails and a delicious food menu. The chic décor and friendly staff make it a popular spot for both expats and locals.

7. Heart of Darkness Craft Brewery

Location: 31D Lý Tự Trọng, Bến Nghé, District 1

Phone Number: +84 28 6656 9098

Heart of Darkness is a craft brewery that offers a variety of unique beers. With its laid-back atmosphere and excellent brews, it's a great place to unwind.

8. Lush

Location: 2 Lý Tự Trọng, District 1

Phone Number: +84 28 3824 2496

Lush is a trendy nightclub that features a lively atmosphere with DJs playing the latest hits. It's a go-to spot for those looking to dance the night away.

9. Tê Tê TapHouse

Location: 90 Nguyễn Huệ, District 1

Phone Number: +84 28 3821 2211

Tê Tê TapHouse is a small yet vibrant bar known for its craft beers. It's a great place to meet friends and enjoy a relaxed evening.

10. Chill Skybar

Location: AB Tower, 76A Lê Lai, District 1

Phone Number: +84 28 3827 2372

Chill Skybar offers a luxurious rooftop bar experience with stunning views of Ho Chi Minh City. It's the perfect place for a glamorous night out, with a great selection of drinks and music.

NIGHTCLUBS AND LIVE MUSIC VENUES

1. Lush Nightclub

Lush Nightclub, situated in the heart of District 1, is one of Ho Chi Minh City's most renowned nightlife attractions. With a combination of foreign DJs and local talent, it provides an upbeat atmosphere ideal for dancing the night away.

Address: District 1, Ho Chi Minh City, 2 Ly Tu Trong

Phone: +84 28 3824 2496.

2. The observatory

The Observatory is noted for its innovative electronic music and breathtaking rooftop vistas. Located in District 4, this venue draws a mixed crowd and presents both local and international DJs.

Address: Ho Chi Minh City, District 4, 5 Nguyen Tat Thanh

Phone number: +84 28 3822 2898.

3. Sax and Art Jazz Club

Sax N' Art Jazz Club is a one-of-a-kind experience for jazz aficionados, with live performances every night. Located in the bustling District 1, it's a nice venue to hear some of the best jazz music in town.

Address: District 1, Ho Chi Minh City, 28 Le Loi

Phone number: +84 28 3822 8472.

4. Yoko Café

Yoko Café is a popular spot among locals due to its cozy environment and unique mix of live music. From rock to indie and everything in between, this District 3 treasure has something for everyone.

Address: Ho Chi Minh City, District 3, 22A Nguyen Thi Dieu

Phone number: +84 28 3933 0577.

5. Acoustic Bar

Acoustic Bar, located in District 3, is a paradise for live music enthusiasts. This venue is well-known for its lively ambiance and outstanding performers, as well as its diverse genre offerings.

Address: District 3, Ho Chi Minh City, 6E1 Ngo Thoi Nhiem

Phone: +84 28 3930 2239.

6. Apocalypse Now

Apocalypse Now, a fixture in Ho Chi Minh City's nightlife, has been entertaining audiences for decades. This District 1 bar, which combines dance music and live acts, is popular with both locals and tourists.

Address: 2B-C-D Thi Sach, District 1, Ho Chi Minh City

Phone number: +84 28 3825 6124.

7. Glow Skybar

Glow Skybar is a trendy rooftop venue in District 1 with spectacular views of the metropolitan skyline. With a combination of live DJ sets and special events, it's ideal for a sophisticated night out.

Address: District 1, Ho Chi Minh City, 93 Nguyen Du

Phone: +84 28 3823 3968.

8. Hard Rock Café

Hard Rock Cafe Ho Chi Minh City, located in the center of District 1, serves delicious food and has live music performances. It features both local and international musicians, making for an amazing rock 'n' roll experience.

Address: District 1, Ho Chi Minh City, 39 Le Duan

Phone number: +84 28 6291 7595.

9. Republic Club in District 1 is well-known for its energetic dance floor and talented DJs. It's a modern venue that draws a hip crowd eager to dance to the latest tunes.

Address: 19 Do Quang Dau, District 1, Ho Chi Minh City

Phone: +84 28 3920 1055.

10. Broma: not a bar.

This unique establishment, which combines live music with rooftop views, is popular with both locals and foreigners. Broma, located in District 1, offers a relaxing atmosphere with an eclectic music selection.

Address: 41 Nguyen Hue, Ho Chi Minh City's District 1.

Phone number: +84 28 3823 6838

THEATERS AND CINEMAS

1. CGV Cinema Liberty Hoang Van Thu

Location: Tan Binh District

Address: 878 Hoang Van Thu Street, Ward 4, Tan Binh District, Ho Chi Minh City

CGV Liberty Hoang Van Thu is a popular choice for moviegoers looking for the latest blockbuster releases in a comfortable setting. This cinema boasts multiple screens, modern sound systems, and a variety of seating options.

2. Galaxy Cinema Nguyen Du

Location: District 1

Address: 116 Nguyen Du Street, Ben Thanh Ward, District 1, Ho Chi Minh City

Located in the heart of the city, Galaxy Cinema Nguyen Du offers a central location for catching the latest films. It features advanced projection technology and comfortable seating, making it a favorite among locals.

3. Lotte Cinema Cantavil

Location: District 2

Address: Cantavil Premier, 1 Song Hanh Street, An Phu Ward, District 2, Ho Chi Minh City

Situated in the upscale area of District 2, Lotte Cinema Cantavil provides a luxurious movie-watching experience. With its modern facilities and variety of snack options, it's an ideal spot for a relaxed evening out.

4. BHD Star Cineplex Icon 68

Location: District 1

Address: District 1, Ben Nghe Ward, 2 Hai Trieu Street, Ho Chi Minh City

BHD Star Cineplex Icon 68 is housed within the iconic Bitexco Financial Tower. It offers stunning views of the city skyline and a wide range of films, from international blockbusters to local Vietnamese movies.

5. CineStar Hai Ba Trung

Location: District 3

Address: 271 Nguyen Trai Street, Ward 5, District 3, Ho Chi Minh City

Known for its cozy atmosphere and friendly service, CineStar Hai Ba Trung provides an intimate setting for movie lovers. It's a great place to watch both mainstream and independent films.

6. Mega GS Cinemas

Location: District 1

Address: 19 Cao Thang Street, Ward 2, District 1, Ho Chi Minh City

Mega GS Cinemas offers a mix of modern amenities and comfortable seating, making it a go-to spot for catching the latest movies. It's conveniently located in District 1, ensuring easy access for city dwellers.

7. Cinebox 212

Location: District 3

Address: 212 Ly Chinh Thang Street, Ward 9, District 3, Ho Chi Minh City

Cinebox 212 is a beloved cinema in District 3, known for its affordable ticket prices and wide selection of films. It's a perfect destination for a casual movie night with friends or family.

8. Saigon Opera House (Municipal Theatre)

Location: District 1

Address: Ben Nghe Ward, District 1, 7 Cong Truong Lam Son, Ho Chi Minh City

For those interested in live performances, the Saigon Opera House is a must-visit. There are many different events held in this magnificent French colonial structure, such as ballet, opera, and traditional Vietnamese shows.

9. The Factory Contemporary Arts Centre

Location: District 2

Address: District 2, Thao Dien Ward, 15 Nguyen U Di Street, Ho Chi Minh City

While primarily an art space, The Factory also screens independent films and documentaries. It's an excellent venue for those looking to explore the intersection of visual arts and cinema.

10. Crescent Mall Cinema

Location: District 7

Address: 101 Ton Dat Tien Street, Tan Phu Ward, District 7, Ho Chi Minh City

Located within the bustling Crescent Mall, this cinema offers a modern movie-going experience with state-of-the-art screens and sound systems. It's a convenient option for residents in the southern part of the city.

NIGHT MARKETS AND EVENING ACTIVITIES

Ben Thanh Night Market

Ben Thanh Market is one of Ho Chi Minh City's most popular night marketplaces. By day, it's a thriving market where you can buy everything from fresh food to souvenirs. At night, it morphs into a bustling street food wonderland. The market stalls spread into the adjacent streets, selling a variety of local foods. From pho to banh mi, fresh seafood to exotic fruits, the options are limitless. The market also sells a variety of handicrafts, apparel, and accessories. Haggling is part of the experience, so don't be afraid to negotiate pricing.

Bui Vien Street

For those seeking a more upbeat atmosphere, Bui Vien Street in the Backpacker District is the place to go. This busy boulevard is studded with bars, nightclubs, and restaurants. Live music, street performers, and a mix of locals and tourists create a lively scene. The street food here is extensive, ranging from grilled meats to vegan selections. It's the ideal place to have a drink, meet new people, and dance the night away.

Nguyen Hue Walking Street

Nguyen Hue Walking Street provides a more family-friendly atmosphere. This pedestrian-only strip is studded with cafés, boutiques, and cultural attractions. On the nights, it transforms into a lively gathering spot with music, dancing performances, and light displays. The colonial architecture, mixed with modern buildings, provides a breathtaking backdrop. It's a nice area to take a stroll, eat ice cream, and people-watch.

Saigon River Dinner Cruises

A dinner cruise on the Saigon River is a great way to unwind. These cruises provide a unique view of the city's skyline lighted against the night sky. While floating along the river, you can enjoy a lunch featuring both local and international food. The pleasant breeze and city lights reflected on the river make for a romantic and memorable experience.

Street Food Tours

A street food tour is a great way to discover the gastronomic wonders of Ho Chi Minh City. These trips, led by local experts, will take you to both hidden gems and major tourist destinations. You'll get to try a variety of meals, learn about their origins, and watch how they're made. It's a unique way to immerse yourself in the city's cuisine culture and uncover dishes you wouldn't have discovered otherwise.

Nighttime Motorcycle Tours

A nocturnal motorbike trip is an exciting way to view the city. While zipping around the streets on the back of a motorcycle, you'll tour several neighborhoods, view renowned landmarks, and stop at local cafes. The chilly night air and the city's bright bustle combine for an exciting ride.

Live Music and Performance

Ho Chi Minh City boasts a robust live music scene. From jazz clubs to rock bars, traditional Vietnamese music to contemporary performances, there is something for everyone. Check out Sax n' Art Jazz Club or Acoustic Bar for a fun night of music and atmosphere.

Night Markets beyond Ben Thanh.

While Ben Thanh is the most well-known, there are several more night markets worth seeing. The Tan Dinh Market and Ky Hoa Night Market provide a more local experience. These marketplaces are less touristy and offer an authentic peek into daily life in the city. You will find a variety of goods, including fresh vegetables, household items, and, of course, wonderful street food.

CHAPTER 9

DAY TRIPS AND EXCURSIONS

MEKONG DELTA

Getting There

To make the most of your day, get started early. Many excursions pick you up from your accommodation in Ho Chi Minh City at around 7 a.m. The bus ride to the Mekong Delta takes around two to three hours, and along the route, you may see rural Vietnam for yourself. As you leave the city behind, the terrain gradually transforms into beautiful farmland and serene streams.

First stop: My Tho.

My Tho, a lively town in the Mekong Delta, is frequently the first destination. You can see the Vinh Trang Pagoda, a stunning temple with exquisite construction and lovely gardens. The pagoda is a peaceful location, ideal for a morning stroll and quiet thought.

Boat Ride on the Mekong River

Next, board a boat and explore the Mekong River. The boat ride is a highlight of the vacation, providing a unique glimpse into life on the river. You will pass by floating marketplaces, where locals sell fruits, vegetables, and other items directly from their boats. These markets are vibrant and bright, highlighting the daily business that keeps the river communities going.

Local Workshops and Villages

Many excursions include stops at local workshops and communities. You may visit a coconut candy workshop to discover how this sweet delight is prepared, or a bee farm to sample fresh honey. These trips offer insight into the traditional crafts and livelihoods of the region's population.

Lunch & Local Cuisine

Lunch is often eaten in a local restaurant, which is often placed in a beautiful garden or by the river. The food of the Mekong Delta is fresh and tasty, including dishes such as elephant ear fish, spring rolls, and other tropical fruits. Trying the local cuisine is a lovely way to discover the region's gastronomic heritage.

Explore the Canals

After lunch, continue your trip by taking a sampan through the small canals. These small, paddle-powered boats go through rivers bordered with lush foliage. The tranquil voyage through the canals provides an opportunity to unwind and enjoy the Delta's natural splendor.

Visiting Fruit Orchards

The Mekong Delta is known for its fruit orchards. A visit to one of these orchards allows you to sample unusual fruits like rambutan, dragon fruit, and longan straight from the tree. Many orchards feature little cafes where you may get fresh fruit juice and snacks.

Return to Ho Chi Minh City

As the day winds down, you'll return to Ho Chi Minh City, usually arriving in the early evening. The trip return provides an opportunity to reflect on the day's events as well as the Mekong Delta's rich culture and natural beauty.

Tips for a Wonderful Day Trip

1. Dress comfortably: Lightweight clothing and comfy shoes are appropriate for the warm, humid weather.

2. Stay Hydrated: Bring a water bottle to stay hydrated all day.

3. Camera Ready: There are plenty of photo opportunities, so keep your camera or smartphone nearby.

4. Respect Local Customs: Be aware of local customs and traditions, especially while visiting temples and rural areas.

5. Travel Light: Pack a small backpack with essentials such as sunscreen, a hat, and insect repellent.

CU CHI TUNNELS

The Cu Chi Tunnels are roughly 40 miles northwest of Ho Chi Minh City, making them ideal for a day trip. Viet Cong forces used these underground tunnels as hiding places, supply routes, hospitals, and housing quarters during the conflict. Today, they are a tribute to the Vietnamese people's inventiveness and determination.

The most convenient way to visit the Cu Chi Tunnels is to take a guided trip. These trips usually include transportation, a skilled guide, and sometimes lunch. If you prefer to go independently, you can rent a car or take the bus from Ho Chi Minh City. The travel takes approximately an hour and a half.

When you arrive, you'll be shown a brief film that explains the history and significance of the tunnels. This sets the tone for the remainder of your trip, allowing you to comprehend the context of what you're about to witness. Following the film, you will have the opportunity to tour the tunnels yourself. Keep in mind that these tunnels are narrow and can seem claustrophobic, however there are bigger areas for individuals who find the cramped conditions bothersome.

One of the tour's highlights is witnessing the numerous traps and weapons utilized by the Viet Cong. These exhibitions show the soldiers' inventiveness as well as the problems they experienced while navigating the area during the conflict. Reconstructed living quarters, kitchens, and conference spaces create a realistic depiction of underground life.

A visit to the Cu Chi Tunnels is about more than simply the tunnels. The surrounding area is lush with flora, providing a pleasant contrast to the site's harsh history. Many excursions include a visit to a local farm or village where you can learn more about Vietnamese daily life during the war.

Before you leave, be sure to sample some of the local cuisine. Traditional Vietnamese delicacies such as pho and banh mi are available in adjacent restaurants, providing a taste of the local cuisine. Many excursions also include the opportunity to sample food that troops would have eaten, such as boiled cassava coated in a peanut-salt combination.

When planning your trip, make sure to dress comfortably and wear strong shoes because you'll be walking a lot. Bring a hat and sunscreen to protect your skin from the sun, and consider carrying a bottle of water to stay hydrated.

Visiting the Cu Chi Tunnels is a dramatic event that provides a fresh perspective on the Vietnam War. It's an opportunity to learn about history in a highly intimate way by witnessing firsthand the conditions that soldiers faced and the techniques they used. Whether you're a history buff or just want to learn more about Vietnam's past, a day trip to the Cu Chi Tunnels is an experience you won't forget.

VUNG TAU BEACH

Getting To Vung Tau

Vung Tau is conveniently located 60 miles southeast of Ho Chi Minh City, making it an ideal day trip destination. You have a few alternatives for getting there:

By Ferry: The fastest method to go to Vung Tau is to take a ferry from Bach Dang Pier in District 1. The cruise lasts approximately 1.5 hours and provides stunning views of the Saigon River and shoreline.

By Bus: Several bus companies provide service from Ho Chi Minh City to Vung Tau. The travel takes between 2 and 2.5 hours, depending on traffic.

By Car: If you want more flexibility, renting a car or using a taxi may be an excellent option. Usually, the drive takes two hours or so.

Explore Vung Tau Beach

When you arrive at Vung Tau, you'll discover plenty of activities and sites to enjoy. Here are a few highlights.

Front Beach (Bai Truoc): This beach, located in the heart of the city, is recognized for its tranquil waters and shaded trees. It's an ideal location for a stroll or a picnic.

Back Beach (Bai Sa): Back Beach, a lengthier stretch of sandy coastline, is ideal for swimming and sunbathing. The waves are mild, making them suitable for families with children.

Pineapple Beach (Bai Dua): This little beach provides a more private setting. It's an ideal location for anyone wishing to avoid the throng.

Must-See Attractions

Vung Tau has a few sites worth visiting:

This magnificent figure of Jesus Christ, which rises atop Small Mountain, is one of Asia's largest. Climb the 800 steps to the top for a spectacular view of the city and coast.

Vung Tau Lighthouse: Built by the French in 1862, this lighthouse offers a panoramic view of the surrounding area. It's a short climb up, but the views are worth it.

Nghinh Phong Cape: This famous destination, known as the "Cape of Welcoming Breeze," is known for its magnificent cliffs and breathtaking ocean vistas. It's an excellent destination for photography aficionados.

White Palace (Bach Dinh): This historic home, built as a summer residence for French governors, is now a museum displaying antiques from the French colonial period.

Local cuisine

No vacation to Vung Tau is complete without trying the local cuisine. Seafood is a highlight here, with various coastal restaurants serving up fresh catch of the day. Don't skip meals like grilled squid, fried fish, and crab soup. For a sweet treat, try the local delicacy, banh khot, which is savory tiny pancakes topped with shrimp and spices.

Practical Tips

Vung Tau is a popular weekend destination, so going on a weekday will help you avoid the throng.

November to April, during the dry season, is the ideal time to come. Remember to bring sunscreen, a hat, and lots of drinks to stay hydrated.

Currency: While most shops accept credit cards, it's a good idea to have some Vietnamese Dong on hand for modest transactions and street food vendors.

CAN GIO BIOSPHERE RESERVE

Getting There

Traveling to Can Gio is an experience in itself. From the Ben Thanh Market area, you have two options: a more pleasant taxi journey or a bus. The journey is made more charming by the drive's picturesque scenery, which includes a ferry ride over the Saigon River.

Exploration of Mangrove Forests

Can Gio's vast mangrove forest, designated as a UNESCO Biosphere Reserve, is one of its main attractions. A boat journey through the thick mangroves provides an exceptional viewpoint of this important environment. A wide range of fauna, including crocodiles, monkeys, and several bird species, can be found in the forest. These tours are educational and entertaining, with guides offering detailed information about the local flora and fauna.

Island of Monkeys

Within the reserve, Monkey Island, also known as Dao Khi, is a must-see. Hundreds of monkeys live on the island, as the name would imply. It's possible to see these entertaining animals in their natural environment, but because monkeys can be mischievous, it's important to keep your stuff safe. You'll come across additional fauna and breathtaking vistas of the surroundings when strolling around the island.

Sanctuary for Crocodiles

The crocodile refuge at Can Gio is another interesting location. This area gives you a close-up look at these prehistoric reptiles. You can add an extra thrill to your stay by feeding the crocodiles on some tours. The sanctuary's mission is to provide visitors with an entertaining experience while supporting the protection of these species.

Vam Sat Natural History Site

Within Can Gio, Vam Sat is an ecotourism destination that provides a range of experiences, including fishing, bird viewing, and seeing a bat lagoon. The location offers amenities for a comfortable visit and is kept up nicely. The bird sanctuary is exceptionally striking, especially in the spring when the trees are crowded with birds that are nesting.

Regional cuisine

A visit to Can Gio wouldn't be complete without trying the local food. Fresh seafood is highly prized in the area, and you may find grilled shrimp, fish hotpot, and crab at several eateries. Usually made with products from the area, the cuisine offers a glimpse of the cuisine's rich history.

CHAPTER 10

CULTURAL ETIQUETTE AND TIPS

DO'S AND DON'TS

Do's:

1. Discover the Local Cuisine: For those who love to eat, Ho Chi Minh City is a culinary haven. Taste authentic Vietnamese cuisine such as banh mi, pho, and fresh spring rolls. Be bold and try what the locals suggest when it comes to street food; it's delicious and safe.

2. See Historical Sites: Allocate some time to see sites like the Reunification Palace, the War Remnants Museum, and the Cu Chi Tunnels. These locations are must-see attractions because they provide in-depth historical insights into Vietnam.

3. Learn a Few Basic Vietnamese words: Although English is widely spoken in Ho Chi Minh City, knowing a few basic Vietnamese words such as "hello" (Xin chào), "thank you" (cảm ơn), and "goodbye" (tạm biệt) would go a long way toward demonstrating respect and improving communication.

4. Dress Respectfully: When visiting temples and other places of worship, especially, wear modest clothing to show your respect for local customs. For the hot and muggy weather, light, breathable

clothes are ideal; but, in places of worship, don't forget to cover your knees and shoulders.

5. Use Vinasun or Mai Linh Taxis: Reputable cab companies like Vinasun and Mai Linh are a good way to stay away from scammers. Their fair price and dependability are well-known.

6. Bargain at Markets: Bargaining is commonplace when shopping at neighborhood markets like Ben Thanh Market. Offer half of the asking amount to begin with, then work out a deal. Take pleasure in the process; it's a part of the shopping culture.

7. Remain Hydrated: Always carry a bottle of water with you because the weather in Ho Chi Minh City may be extremely hot. Another hydrated and refreshing option that is widely accessible from street vendors is coconut water.

DON'TS

1. Don't Flash Valuables: In crowded places, petty theft can be a concern. Especially in crowded marketplaces and tourist destinations, keep your valuables hidden, abstain from wearing ostentatious jewelry, and pay attention to your surroundings.

2. Steer clear of sketchy motorbike taxis: Although motorbike taxis (xe om) are a common form of transportation, make sure you utilize a reliable service or have a fare agreed upon before you go. You can make sure you get a fair price and a safer journey by using applications like Grab.

3. Avoid Drinking Tap Water: Use bottled water to rinse your teeth and drink. While ice in beverages at respectable restaurants is usually harmless, it's best to stay on the safe side to prevent any health problems.

4. Refrain from Touching People's Heads: The head is revered as the most sacred portion of the body in Vietnamese culture. To respect regional traditions, refrain from touching anyone's head, even small toddlers.

5. Don't Disregard Traffic Laws: Ho Chi Minh City traffic may be quite hectic. To safely negotiate the busy roads, always check both directions before crossing the street, utilize pedestrian crossings when available, and take the lead from the locals.

6. Don't Point with Your Finger: Make gestures with your entire hand rather than just your finger. In Vietnam, pointing with the finger is frowned upon.

7. Don't Lose Your Temper: It's critical to keep your composure and manners appropriate. It is improper to become overtly irate or to raise your voice in public, and doing so will not address any problems you may be having.

LOCAL CUSTOMS AND TRADITIONS

Respect for the Ancestors and Elders

One of the most important features of Vietnamese society is a strong reverence for ancestors and the elderly. This regard is obvious both in ordinary interactions and on exceptional occasions. When visiting temples or residences, you may observe altars decorated with photographs, incense, and offerings like fruits and flowers. These altars honor ancestors, and a modest bow when passing by is a respectful gesture.

Greetings and Social Etiquette

When meeting someone, a simple bow or nod is a customary greeting. Handshakes are also appropriate, particularly in more formal circumstances. When shaking hands, it is customary to use both hands or support your right forearm with your left. Remember to address people by their titles and surnames, as this shows respect.

For example, Mr. Nguyen would be addressed as "Mr. Nguyen" rather than simply "Nguyen."

Traditional Clothing

While Ho Chi Minh City is a sophisticated city, traditional dress remains crucial for festivals and special events. The "ao dai," or long, graceful tunic worn over trousers, is the national costume and a symbol of Vietnamese grace. Women may wear "ao dai" at Tet (Lunar New Year) or other notable occasions. These outfits are more than just apparel; they express Vietnamese tradition and pride.

Festivals and Celebrations

Ho Chi Minh City is filled with festivities all year, each providing a unique peek into local culture. The most significant holiday is Tet, also known as Lunar New Year. It is a time for family reunions, remembering ancestors, and expressing thanks. The streets are colorfully decked, and there are markets selling flowers, traditional foods, and festive souvenirs.

Another prominent event is the Mid-Autumn Festival, in which children carry lanterns of various shapes and eat mooncakes. These celebrations are not only cheerful but also firmly ingrained in Vietnamese culture, representing the community's values and beliefs.

Food and Dining Etiquette

Vietnamese cuisine is a highlight of any trip to Ho Chi Minh City. Sharing meals helps to strengthen social relationships. When dining with locals, you'll observe that meals are served family-style, with everyone sharing communal plates. It is traditional to wait for the oldest person to start eating before you begin. It's also crucial to handle chopsticks appropriately; never stick them vertically in a bowl of rice, as this resembles incense sticks used in funeral rites.

Market Culture

Markets are the lifeblood of Ho Chi Minh City, selling everything from fresh fruit to handcrafted items. Ben Thanh Market is one of the most well-known, where you may witness the hustle and bustle of local trade. Haggling is normal, and it's a good method to communicate with sellers. Approach bargaining with a nice attitude and a grin; the social contact is just as important as the ultimate price.

Public Conduct

Respect and civility are crucial in public areas. Avoid raising your voice or displaying excessive affection, as these actions can be interpreted as contempt. Dress modestly when visiting religious locations, covering your shoulders and knees, and always take off your shoes before entering a temple or someone's home.

ESSENTIAL VIETNAMESE PHRASES

Basic Greetings

Understanding basic greetings is the first step to connecting with locals. Here are some essential phrases:

Hello: "Xin chào" (sin chow)

Goodbye: "Tạm biệt" (tam byet)

Thank you: "Cảm ơn" (kahm uhn)

Yes: "Vâng" (vuhng)

No: "Không" (kohng)

Polite Phrases

Politeness is appreciated in any culture, and Vietnam is no different. Here are some polite phrases that will help you in various situations:

Please: "Làm ơn" (lahm uhn)

Excuse me / Sorry: "Xin lỗi" (sin loy)

No problem: "Không sao" (kohng sao)

Directions and Transportation

Getting around Ho Chi Minh City can be overwhelming, but these phrases will help you ask for directions and navigate transportation:

Where is...?: "Ở đâu...?" (uh dow)

How much is the fare?: "Giá vé bao nhiêu?" (zah vay bow nyew)

Bus: "Xe buýt" (seh buýt)

Taxi: "Taxi" (tahk-see)

Hotel: "Khách sạn" (khak san)

Dining Out

Ho Chi Minh City is a food lover's paradise. Knowing some food-related phrases will enhance your dining experience:

Menu: "Thực đơn" (thook dohn)

Water: "Nước" (nuhk)

Delicious: "Ngon" (ngon)

Check, please: "Tính tiền" (ting tien)

Vegetarian: "Ăn chay" (ahn chai)

Shopping

Whether you're at a bustling market or a modern shopping center, these phrases will help you with your purchases:

How much?: "Bao nhiêu?" (bow nyew)

Expensive: "Đắt" (daht)

Cheap: "Rẻ" (reh)

I want to buy this: "Tôi muốn mua cái này" (toy moon moo-ah kai nai)

Emergencies

In case of emergencies, it's crucial to know these phrases:

Help!: "Cứu!" (ku)

I need a doctor: "Tôi cần bác sĩ" (toy kun bahk see)

Call the police: "Gọi cảnh sát" (goy cang saht)

Tips for Using Vietnamese Phrases

1. Pronunciation Matters: Vietnamese is a tonal language, meaning the pitch at which a word is spoken can change its meaning. Listening to locals and mimicking their intonation can help you get it right.

2. Practice with Locals: Don't be afraid to practice your Vietnamese with locals. Most people will appreciate your effort and help you improve.

3. Carry a Phrasebook: While smartphones are handy, having a small phrasebook can be a lifesaver in areas with poor reception or when your battery dies.

4. Be Patient and Smile: Patience and a friendly demeanor go a long way. If you're struggling with a phrase, a smile and a positive attitude can help bridge the communication gap.

CHAPTER 11

PRACTICAL INFORMATION

CURRENCY AND BANKING

Currency

Vietnam's official currency is the Vietnamese Dong (VND). While US dollars are occasionally accepted in tourist destinations, it is normally preferable to use local money. Bills are issued in a variety of denominations, the most frequent being 1,000, 2,000, 5,000, 10,000, 20,000, 50,000, 100,000, 200,000, and 500,000 VND. Smaller denominations (less than 1,000 VND) are rarely used.

Exchange Rates

To secure a fair deal, remain up to date on the current currency rate. Rates fluctuate, so verify them before exchanging money. According to recent values, $1 USD is equivalent to around 23,000 VND, though this might vary.

Where To Exchange Money

There are various methods for converting currency in Ho Chi Minh City:

Banks provide dependable exchange rates and are a safe way to exchange money. Most banks in Ho Chi Minh City are open from

8:00 a.m. to 4:00 p.m., Monday through Friday, with some open on Saturday mornings.

Currency exchange counters are typically found at airports, major hotels, and retail malls. Although convenient, they may provide slightly lower interest rates than banks.

ATMs: ATMs are widely distributed around the city and frequently offer a decent exchange rate. However, you should be mindful of potential fees from both your home bank and the local ATM operator.

Using Credit and Debit Cards

Credit and debit cards are generally accepted in hotels, restaurants, and larger retail stores. Visa and MasterCard are the most widely accepted, however, American Express and other cards may be less so. It's a good idea to carry some cash for little transactions, street food, and establishments that don't accept credit cards.

Banking Services

Ho Chi Minh City is home to a large number of local and foreign banks. Some of the prominent banks are:

Vietcombank BIDV

VietinBank Agribank

HSBC ANZ

These banks provide a wide range of services, including basic currency exchange and more complex financial services.

Opening Hours

Banks are normally open from 8:00 AM to 4:00 PM, Monday through Friday. Some branches are open on Saturday mornings, though this varies. It is a good idea to check the branch's hours ahead of time.

Tips for Safe Banking

1. Use reputable banks and ATMs. To avoid card skimming devices or scams, stick to well-known banks and ATMs.

2. Notify your bank. Before leaving, notify your bank of your vacation to avoid having your card stopped for suspicious behavior.

3. Keep Cash Secure: Carry only what you need for the day and store the remainder in your hotel safe.

HEALTH AND SAFETY TIPS

1. Stay hydrated and eat safely.

The tropical environment in Ho Chi Minh City may be hot and humid, so staying hydrated is crucial. Consume plenty of bottled water and avoid tap water. When it comes to food, street vendors serve tasty and genuine Vietnamese cuisine, but it is best to dine at booths that appear clean and have a significant turnover of people. This typically signifies fresh food.

2. Be cautious with your belongings.

Petty theft can be a concern in popular tourist destinations. Use a money belt or a cross-body bag to keep your stuff secure and in front of you. Avoid showcasing high-end things like jewelry, cameras, and cell phones. When wearing a backpack, ensure that it is secure and consider utilizing a lock.

3. Use Reliable Transportation.

Ho Chi Minh City offers a variety of transportation alternatives, including buses, cabs, and motorcycles. For safety, use reliable taxi companies such as Vinasun or Mai Linh, who are known for their dependability. If you prefer to use ride-hailing applications, Grab is a popular and safe choice in the city.

4. Be aware of traffic.

Traffic in Ho Chi Minh City can be intimidating, with motorcycles flying around in all directions. When crossing the street, walk slowly and steadily, keeping eye contact with approaching automobiles. They're used to navigating around pedestrians. If you opt to rent a motorcycle, make sure to wear a helmet.

5. Protect yourself from the sun and mosquitos.

The sun can be fairly harsh, so protect yourself with sunscreen, a hat, and sunglasses. Mosquitoes can spread diseases such as dengue fever, therefore wear insect repellent, particularly in the early morning and late afternoon. If you'll be in an area with a lot of mosquitos, consider wearing long sleeves and pants.

6. Know the emergency numbers.

In the event of an emergency, it is critical to know the local emergency numbers. In Vietnam, the general emergency numbers are 113 for police, 114 for firefighters, and 115 for ambulances. Keep these numbers handy during your journey.

7. Respect local customs and laws.

Understanding and following local norms and regulations can help you avoid misunderstandings. Dress modestly, particularly when visiting religious sites. When you enter a temple or someone's home, take off your shoes. Learning a few simple Vietnamese words is also an excellent way to show respect.

8. Stay connected.

Having a local SIM card can be quite handy for navigation and communication with others. You may easily get a SIM card at the airport or in the city. Make sure your phone is unlocked before your journey.

9. Health precautions.

Before flying, see your doctor to ensure you are up to date on your immunizations. Carry a basic first-aid kit with you, including any prescription prescriptions you may require. Be aware of the nearest medical facilities in case you require medical assistance.

10. Travel insurance.

Travel insurance can provide you peace of mind during your journey. It can provide coverage for unexpected events such as medical emergencies, vacation cancellations, and missing luggage. Make sure you select a comprehensive plan that meets your travel needs.

INTERNET AND SIM CARDS

Understanding Mobile Networks

Ho Chi Minh City, like the rest of Vietnam, has a robust and reliable mobile network infrastructure. Viettel, Vinaphone, and MobiFone are some of the major telecom operators. These companies offer a selection of prepaid SIM cards tailored to tourists, with bundles that include data, calls, and messages.

Purchase a SIM Card

Once you arrive in Ho Chi Minh City, you may easily acquire a SIM card. The easiest place to buy one is at Tan Son Nhat International Airport, where kiosks are located in the arrivals area. SIM cards are also available at local convenience stores, mobile phone shops, and official telecom provider outlets across the city.

Required Documentation

To purchase a SIM card, you must give your passport for registration. This method guarantees that local standards are followed while also protecting your personal information.

Choosing the Right Plan

When choosing a SIM card, consider how much data you'll use. If you want to use your phone solely for navigation, social networking, and occasional surfing, a data package of 3-5 GB should be sufficient for a week-long trip. For people who require constant internet connectivity, search for unlimited data plans or those with greater data restrictions.

Set up your SIM card

Once you've acquired your SIM card, the vendor will normally assist you in installing and activating it. They can also help you set up your phone to guarantee it works properly. Before you travel, make sure your phone is unlocked and compatible with local networks.

Accessing Wi-Fi

Wi-Fi is generally available throughout Ho Chi Minh City. Most hotels, cafes, restaurants, and public venues provide free Wi-Fi to their clients. It's a good idea to ask for the Wi-Fi password anytime you stop for a coffee or a meal because it can help you conserve bandwidth.

Staying Secure Online

It is critical to maintain security when utilizing public Wi-Fi. Avoid accessing sensitive information, such as online banking or personal accounts, via unprotected networks. A Virtual Private Network (VPN) can provide an additional degree of security by safeguarding your data from potential attacks.

Tips for Staying Connected

1. Keep Your SIM Card and Passport Handy: Always keep your SIM card information and passport on hand in case you need to top up or handle any issues.

2. Use Messaging Apps: WhatsApp, Viber, and Facebook Messenger are popular in Vietnam. These applications are ideal for staying in touch with other travelers and making new acquaintances along the road.

3. Monitor Your Data Usage: Keep track of how much data you use to avoid running out suddenly. Most cellphone companies provide apps or services for checking your remaining balance and data.

4. Consider a Portable Wi-Fi Device: If you require consistent and reliable internet connectivity for many devices, renting a portable Wi-Fi device may be a viable alternative. These devices are available for hire at the airport or from a variety of internet vendors.

CONCLUSION

As we conclude this 2024 travel guide to Ho Chi Minh City's colorful streets and quiet rivers, we hope you are as inspired as we are to explore the city's rich tapestry of culture, history, and modernity. From the busy markets of Ben Thanh to the tranquil corridors of the War Remnants Museum, each chapter of our guide has attempted to convey the essence of Saigon's energy and the friendliness of its people.

Ho Chi Minh City is a destination where the past and present blend harmoniously, allowing tourists to dig into its legendary history while seeing the rapid rise of a bustling metropolis. Whether you've tasted the flavors of street food favorites like pho and banh mi or gazed at the city skyline from the Saigon Skydeck, every moment in this city promises a mix of discovery and delight.

For those looking for adventure, the adjacent Mekong Delta provides a spectacular journey through Vietnam's agricultural heartland, complete with floating marketplaces and scenic vistas. For urban explorers, the city's myriad cafes, galleries, and boutiques provide an abundance of possibilities to immerse themselves in current Vietnamese culture and innovation.

As you near the end of this guide, reflect on not only what you've read, but also how you've felt. If stories about Ho Chi Minh City's resilient, rich culture and hospitable people have piqued your interest, it's time to put that inspiration into action. Plan your trip, pack your bags, and go on an adventure that promises to be as rewarding as it is exciting.

Ho Chi Minh City awaits you not just as a destination, but also as a new chapter in your journey of exploration and discovery. Set out and let every street corner, local smile, and sun-soaked vista inspire you to keep exploring. Saigon is more than just a tourist destination; it's a place to explore, cherish, and remember. So what are you waiting for? The experience of a lifetime starts here, in the heart of Vietnam.

Printed in Great Britain
by Amazon